Robert S. Duncanson
"the spiritual striving of the freedmen's sons"

May 1–October 30, 2011

Joseph D. Ketner II

Thomas Cole National Historic Site
Catskill, New York

This catalogue accompanies the exhibition

Robert S. Duncanson *"the spiritual striving of the freedmen's sons"*

May 1 - October 30, 2011

218 Spring Street, PO Box 426
Catskill, New York 12414
518-943-7465
www.thomascole.org

ISBN: 978-0-9823444-7-7
0-9823444-7-3

On the cover: Robert S, Duncanson, *Summer*, 1849, oil on canvas, 11 ½ × 16 ⅜ inches. Michael Rosenfeld Gallery, LLC, New York, New York.

Director's Foreword

It has been ten years since the opening of the Thomas Cole National Historic Site to the public in July 2001, and it is for this special anniversary year that we present the paintings of Robert S. Duncanson. For both 2010 and 2011, we organized exhibitions that challenged assumptions about 19th century landscape painting, first with an exhibition of women artists of the Hudson River School, followed this year by a pioneering artist of African-American descent. We are proud to host these ground-breaking exhibitions and are delighted with the voluminous press coverage and big increase in attendance, but most of all we are so grateful to the curators who brought their brilliant scholarship to the Thomas Cole site. This year we were lucky enough to attract the attention of Joseph D. Ketner, who has decades of research about Duncanson under his belt, and an enthusiasm for the subject that comes through in everything he does. When our trustee David Barnes first asked Mr. Ketner if he would consider curating a Duncanson show at Thomas Cole's home, he replied "How many ways can I say yes?" Duncanson never exhibited his work on the east coast during his lifetime, and he admired Cole immensely. We are enjoying the thought of how delighted Duncanson might have been to know that his paintings would be on view inside the home of Thomas Cole.

Our annual exhibitions are a team effort, and there are many people to thank for bringing this year's production together. I must here again mention Joseph Ketner, who is such a professional as well as a pleasure to work with. It has been a privilege to learn so much from him. For this beautiful catalogue I'd like to thank Marie Spano for donating her editing skills and to Ron Toelke for his design. Our exhibition sponsors are The Bank of Greene County, The Greene County Legislature through the County Initiative Program administered by the Greene County Council on the Arts, and Greene County Tourism Promotion. Many thanks to Sheri DeJan for assembling all of the high-resolution images for this publication, and to our newest staff member Kate Menconeri for taking over the logistics for this show mid-stream! For the exhibition installation, our thanks go to Patrick Terenchin, who has made each of our shows more stunning than the one before. Many thanks to all of our volunteers who staff the opening events, and to Melissa Gavilanes who organizes them all. Lastly, my thanks to you, our readers and visitors, for supporting the Thomas Cole National Historic Site with your presence and your enthusiasm. I look forward to seeing you here soon and often.

Elizabeth B. Jacks
Executive Director
Thomas Cole National Historic Site

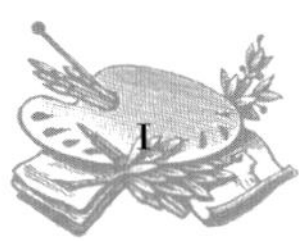

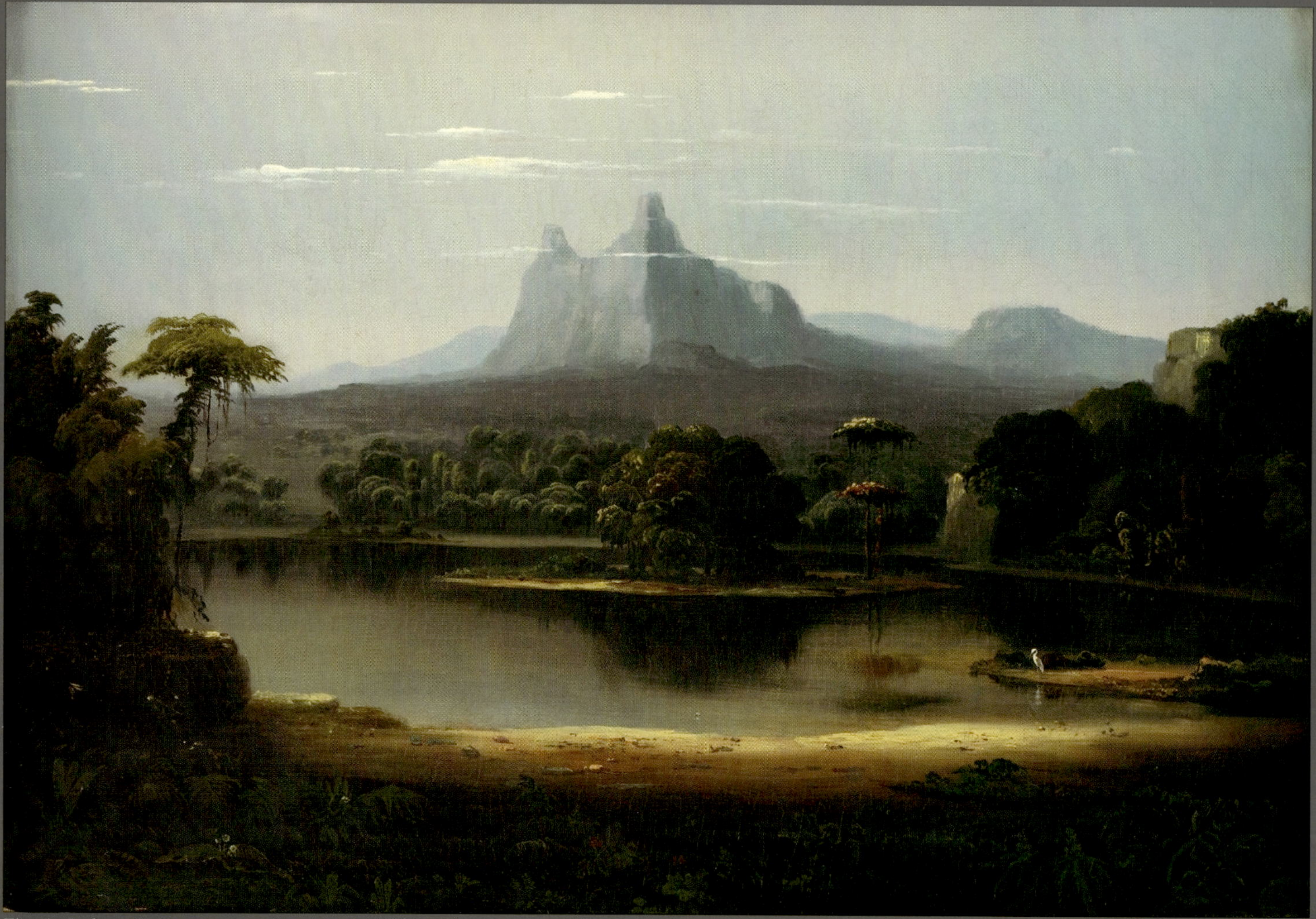

Fig. 1. Robert S. Duncanson, *Landscape*, 1851, oil on canvas, 15 × 22 inches, Collection of the Hunter Museum of American Art, Chattanooga, Tennessee, Museum purchase, HMAA. 2007.6.

Robert S. Duncanson

"the spiritual striving of the freedmen's sons"

— W.E.B. Du Bois[1]

Joseph D. Ketner II
Henry and Lois Foster Chair in Contemporary Art
Emerson College, Boston

Robert S. Duncanson crafted a position as the principal artist from a vibrant group of Ohio River Valley regional landscape painters in the mid-nineteenth century [Fig. 1]. Based in Cincinnati, Ohio, then the largest and most prosperous city in the western United States, he participated in the national fascination with landscape painting and used the North American landscape as a metaphor to express America's cultural identity. Duncanson followed the model of landscape painting established by his predecessors Thomas Cole and Asher B. Durand who, as President of the National Academy of Design, eloquently articulated its ideals in his *Letters on Landscape Painting*, "it is by reverent attention to the realized forms of Nature alone, that Art is enabled by its delegated power to reproduce some measure of the profound and elevated emotions which the contemplation of the visible works of God awaken."[2] Duncanson created pastoral and picturesque views, often imaginary, and strove to elevate landscape painting, in emulation of Durand's words, above a mere depiction of nature to convey grand ideas that would provide moral lessons for the viewer. The regional press heralded Duncanson at the height of his career as "the best landscape painter in the West."[3] His landscape paintings also resonated with international audiences. The art press in Canada and England, where he traveled, held him in especially high esteem. Canadians acknowledged Duncanson's seminal role as "one of the earliest of our professional cultivators of the fine arts."[4] And, critics writing in the *London Art Journal* praised him as possessing "the skill of a master," whose paintings "may compete with any of the modern British school."[5]

Duncanson achieved his artistic success despite the oppressive restrictions under which he worked as an African American, or "free

colored person." Duncanson adopted the style and metaphors of east coast landscape painting, depicting the "natural paradise" of the New World as a romantic symbol for man's relationship with God. Literature on the Hudson River School artists, and the legions of artists that they influenced, discusses the cultural meanings imbedded in their paintings.[6] Duncanson's paintings clearly demonstrate that he too was working in the shadow of Thomas Cole and the Hudson River School. However, because American society identified him as an ethnic minority, discriminated against in law and practice, his circumstances are distinctive among his artistic peers. By working within the idiom of American landscape painting, he appropriated it for African-American culture. And, in some of his paintings, he subtly expressed the distinctive viewpoint of an African American in the antebellum era. This exhibition focuses on the development of Duncanson's career and his art, attempting to interpret the Anglo-American content through the prism of his identity as a mulatto "free colored person."

Duncanson's paintings rarely overtly depict issues that one would expect to have concerned African Americans in the antebellum era, specifically slavery and racial discrimination. Yet, a study of his life reveals that he was actively involved with abolitionists, many of whom patronized him, and he participated in anti-slavery societies. Abolitionist journals across North America championed his numerous efforts on behalf of the anti-slavery movement as well as his artistic accomplishments. The apparent contradictions between his abolitionist stance and his landscape paintings characterize Duncanson's response to the obstacles that confronted an African-American artist working in the antebellum United States.

Duncanson's dilemma epitomizes what African-American intellectual W.E.B. Dubois described as an African American's "double consciousness" where he "ever feels his twoness, — an American, a Negro; two souls, two thoughts, two unreconciled strivings; two warring ideals...." Du Bois also described the "veil" that separates the Euro-American and African-American communities.[7] Faced with marketing his paintings to a predominantly white audience, Duncanson navigated his two cultures by subtly signifying the African-American perspective in some of his paintings. With a careful reading of his landscapes, in the larger context of his career and the social and political events that influenced him, we may be able to peek behind the "veil" and better understand Duncanson's particular perspective as an African-American artist.

When a scholar first discovered a photograph of Duncanson in 1982,[8] the art history community was puzzled. Was this artist, as history had informed us, an African American, or as the title of the accompanying article states a "black" artist? [Fig. 2] If we examine this photograph from a twenty-first century perspective, the sitter appears to be Caucasian. However, from the perspective of nineteenth-century American society, Robert Duncanson was unquestionably an African American. Every census in which his name appears recorded him as a mulatto "free colored person." His patrons, colleagues, abolitionists, journalists, and art critics in the United States, almost without exception, refer to him as the "Negro," "colored," or "mulatto"

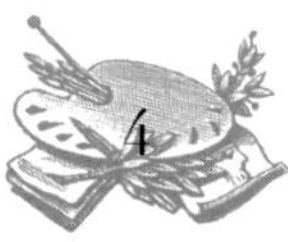

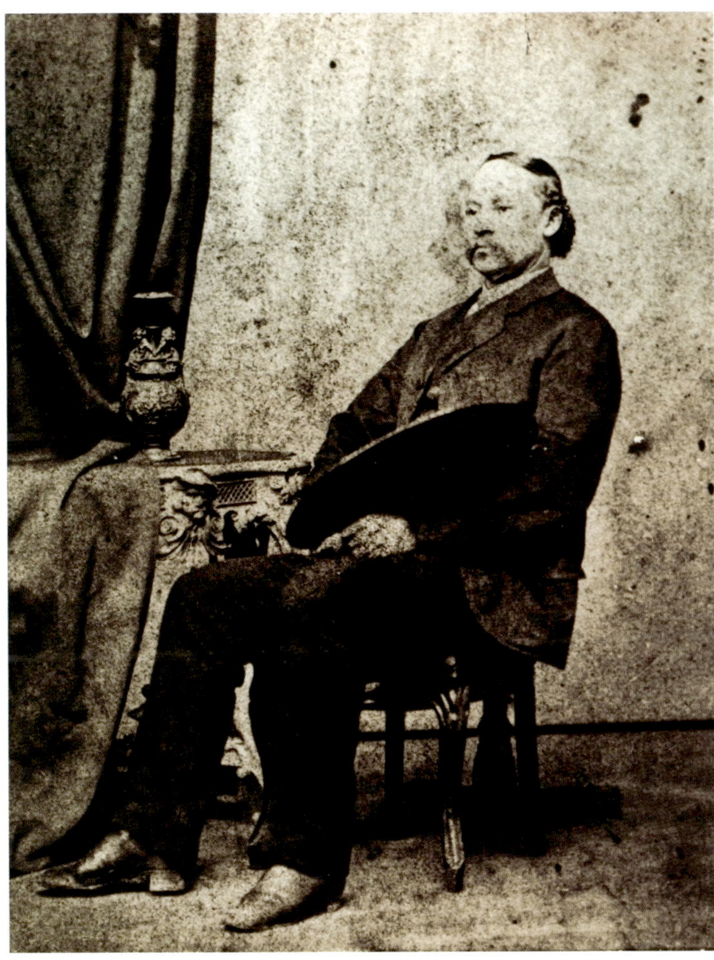

Fig. 2. J. W. Winder, *Robert S. Duncanson,* c. 1868, daguerreotype. Monroe County Historical Museum, Michigan.

artist. Interestingly, when he traveled in Canada, England, and Europe his racial identity is almost never mentioned.

The American public's identification of Duncanson as a "colored" man dictated his social position and the opportunities available to him in the highly stratified antebellum society. The racial prejudice he confronted on a daily basis presented numerous obstacles to his career. Not only did legislated slavery exist but freedmen lived a life variously described as "equal but not free," or "slaves without masters."[9] In the 1830s and 40s, black laws, Jim Crow laws, and social discrimination severely curtailed the activities and opportunities of "free colored persons." In Ohio, where Duncanson lived, "free colored persons" were required to post a $500 bond in order to settle in the state. Significantly, Cincinnati was the site of some of the most severe race riots in the antebellum North.[10]

Robert Duncanson's life unfolded in a scenario typical for a mulatto "free colored person" in antebellum America. His parents John Dean and Lucy, along with his grandparents, moved north to Fayette, New York from their native Virginia around the turn of the nineteenth century. The United States Census lists them as "mulatto" "free colored persons," who worked as carpenters. The Duncanson clan probably benefited from the first mass emancipation of slaves after the American Revolution. The majority of those liberated came from the Upper South (states such as Virginia) and were mulatto slaves, who as offspring of the master often held privileged positions in the slave hierarchy, were taught skills, and were educated. Many of these former slaves moved north, seeking opportunity in northern states that

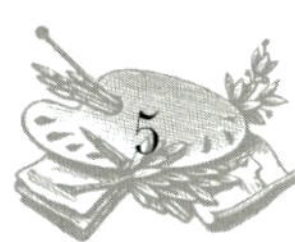

raised in the county of Monroe, $5

Resolved, That the proceedings be published in both papers of this city.

A. G. BATES, Sec'y.

A NEW FIRM.

JOHN GAMBLIN & R. DUNCANSON, PAINTERS AND GLAZIERS, beg leave to acquaint their friends and the citizens of Monroe and its vicinity, that they have established themselves in the above business, and respectfully solicit patronage. They pledge themselves to do work in the most superi r style, and to use the best and genuine materials for the same on the lowest possible terms,—lower than ever executed in this city.

Monroe, April 16, 1838. 32-4w

TO RENT, THE CITY HOTEL, situated on Washington street, in the City of Monroe, formerly owned and kept by P. Spalding, and now owned and kept by the subscriber.

Fig. 3. A NEW FIRM, *Monroe Gazette* (Michigan), April 17, 1838.

had abolished slavery by 1803, in the first massive migration of African Americans to the North. The Duncansons followed this migratory pattern and, in fact, moved into the Central New York Military Tract, where the Federal government located and granted land to Revolutionary War veterans, implying that Duncanson's grandfather, Charles (c. 1744–1828), may have earned his freedom in exchange for military service.[11]

The Duncanson's participated in the growth of the black middle class at the turn of the nineteenth century, a time when African-American artisans predominated in the trades in the United States. Robert Seldon Duncanson was born in 1821 and was mentored in the family trades of carpentry and house painting. Some years after the death of Duncanson's grandfather, the family moved to Monroe, Michigan, then a prosperous community at the tip of Lake Erie. In Monroe, at the age of sixteen, Robert reached the apprentice stage of his training and his father hired him out to a local house painter.[12] From this craftsman Robert would have learned painting, glazing, mixing colors, preparing surfaces, and applying paint. Sufficiently trained in these skills, Duncanson went into business with a partner in 1838 and advertised in the local *Monroe Gazette*, "A NEW FIRM, John Gamblin and R. Duncanson, Painters and Glaziers, beg leave to acquaint their friends and the citizens of Monroe and its vicinity, that they have established themselves in the above business and respectfully solicit patronage." [Fig. 3]

Duncanson was in business for only about a year before the partnership dissolved, and he resolved to become an artist and

to break into the art community, which was almost exclusively Caucasian. An abolitionist journal of the period reported that a friend, perhaps his former partner John Gamblin, encouraged him to paint a portrait, provided the supplies, and thus stimulated Duncanson's artistic ambitions.[13] With encouragement, he moved in 1840 to Cincinnati, then the economic and cultural center of the United States west of the Appalachian Mountains. Equally significant, Cincinnati was also one of the three major population centers for "free colored persons" in America and a stronghold of abolitionist activity.

Living in neighboring Mt. Healthy with family friends,[14] Duncanson observed the active Cincinnati cultural community and taught himself to paint by copying prints, sketching from nature, and painting portraits. Like many artists of this period, economic pressure forced him to become itinerant, traveling across Ohio and Michigan seeking portrait commissions. It was extremely difficult for an African American in an era of "black laws" to secure commissions. However, a few abolitionist sympathizers patronized the artist and by 1846 the *Detroit Daily Advertiser* reported that the young artist painted "portraits...of great merit,"[15] such as the accomplished 1844 *Portrait of William J. Baker* [Fig. 4].

By the end of the 1840s the growing prominence of landscape painting in American art motivated Duncanson, along with William L. Sonntag and Worthington Whittredge, to pursue the genre and paint images of the Ohio River Valley. Instrumental to Duncanson's development was Benjamin McConkey, a pupil of Thomas Cole, who came to Cincinnati in 1847 as Cole's agent to negotiate the sale of

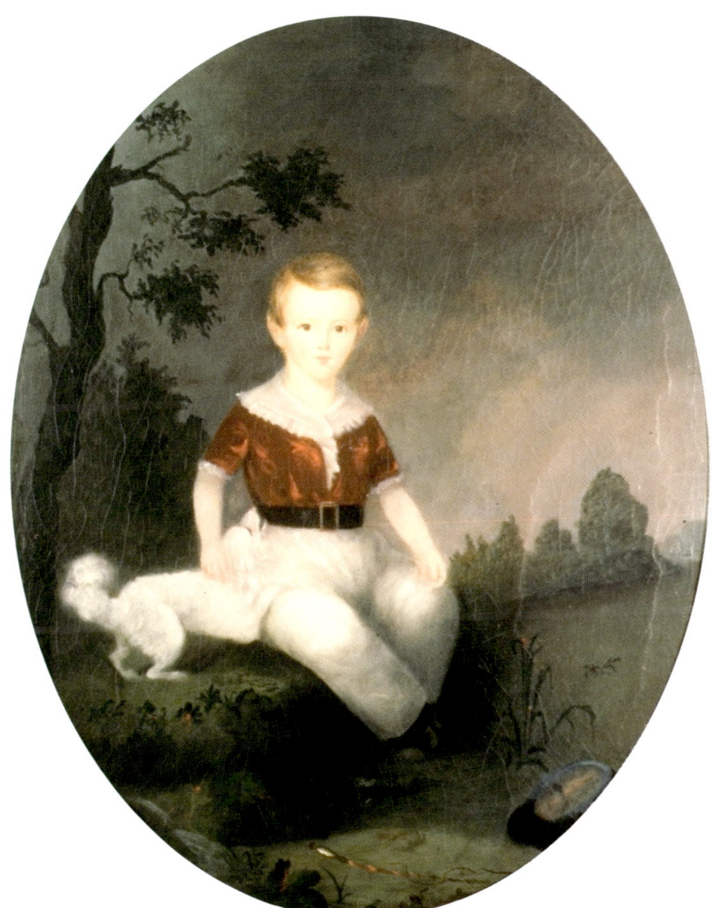

Fig. 4. Robert S. Duncanson, *Portrait of William J. Baker*, 1844, oil on canvas, 27 5/8 × 22 3/4 inches. Baker-Hunt Foundation, Covington, Kentucky.

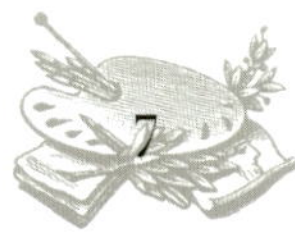

the *Voyage of Life* (1846, National Gallery of Art) through the Western Art Union.[16] The exhibition of Cole's important series on the four stages of life caused a sensation among artists and the public. More important, this episode marks a turning point in Duncanson's artistic development: from this point forward landscape painting was his métier. Cole's influence is evident in Duncanson's *Carp River, Lake Superior* [1850, Fig. 5], in which Duncanson frames a wilderness scene with twisted, decaying trees that suggest the power of nature and the cycle of life. In addition, at this phase of his career, Duncanson expressed his indebtedness to Cole by directly copying his *Dream of Arcadia* [1852, Fig. 6], and *Garden of Eden* [1852, Private Collection]. Working with his colleagues Sonntag and Whittredge under the influence of Cole, Duncanson quickly developed an accomplished style. By the early 1850s he was creating remarkable paintings that captured the picturesque wonders of nature and was contributing to the Euro-American glorification of the North American landscape [Fig. 1].

By painting the picturesque wonders of the North American landscape, Duncanson helped to forge an American cultural identity. He also appropriated these metaphors as part of his African-American cultural heritage. Especially significant in this regard is his *View of Cincinnati, Ohio from Covington, Kentucky* [1851, Fig. 7], in which he depicts the bustling riverfront of Cincinnati with smokestacks spewing and densely packed buildings suggesting the prosperity of the booming city. He copied his composition directly from a print in *Graham's Magazine* from 1848 [Fig. 8]. Since every mark a painter makes on a blank canvas represents either a conscious decision or a conditioned response, the points at which Duncanson's painting digresses from its printed source are significant. The painting nearly replicates the print, but if one compares the figures in the print, all of whom are white, with the figures in the painting, Duncanson has altered this group to depict a black man carrying a scythe (instead of a rifle), a symbol of labor, and a black woman in the background hanging laundry to dry beside a ramshackle cabin. In the distance, on the Kentucky side of the river bank, a white couple leisurely lounges on the hillside enjoying the view of Cincinnati across the river. The African-American artist has poignantly contrasted the free white classes of Kentucky and their laboring black slaves with the prosperity and freedom available just across the river in Ohio. In what appears to be a simple cityscape, Duncanson subtly interjected his commentary condemning the practice of slavery on the Kentucky side of the river. In this painting the Ohio River beckons the black slaves to cross it, like the River Jordan, to freedom and opportunity in Cincinnati and the North.

Duncanson's paintings, however, rarely directly addressed racial oppression, prejudice, and slavery. The only explicitly African-American subject he ever painted was *Uncle Tom and Little Eva* [1853, Fig. 9] painted on commission from an abolitionist minister after Harriet Beecher Stowe's (1811–1896) immensely popular novel *Uncle Tom's Cabin* (1852). Besides this overt treatment of an abolitionist theme, the undercurrent of African-American content in Duncanson's paintings probably went unnoticed by his clientele. It was in fact the extraordinary quality of his work that earned him considerable attention among local patrons and even a commission to paint landscape

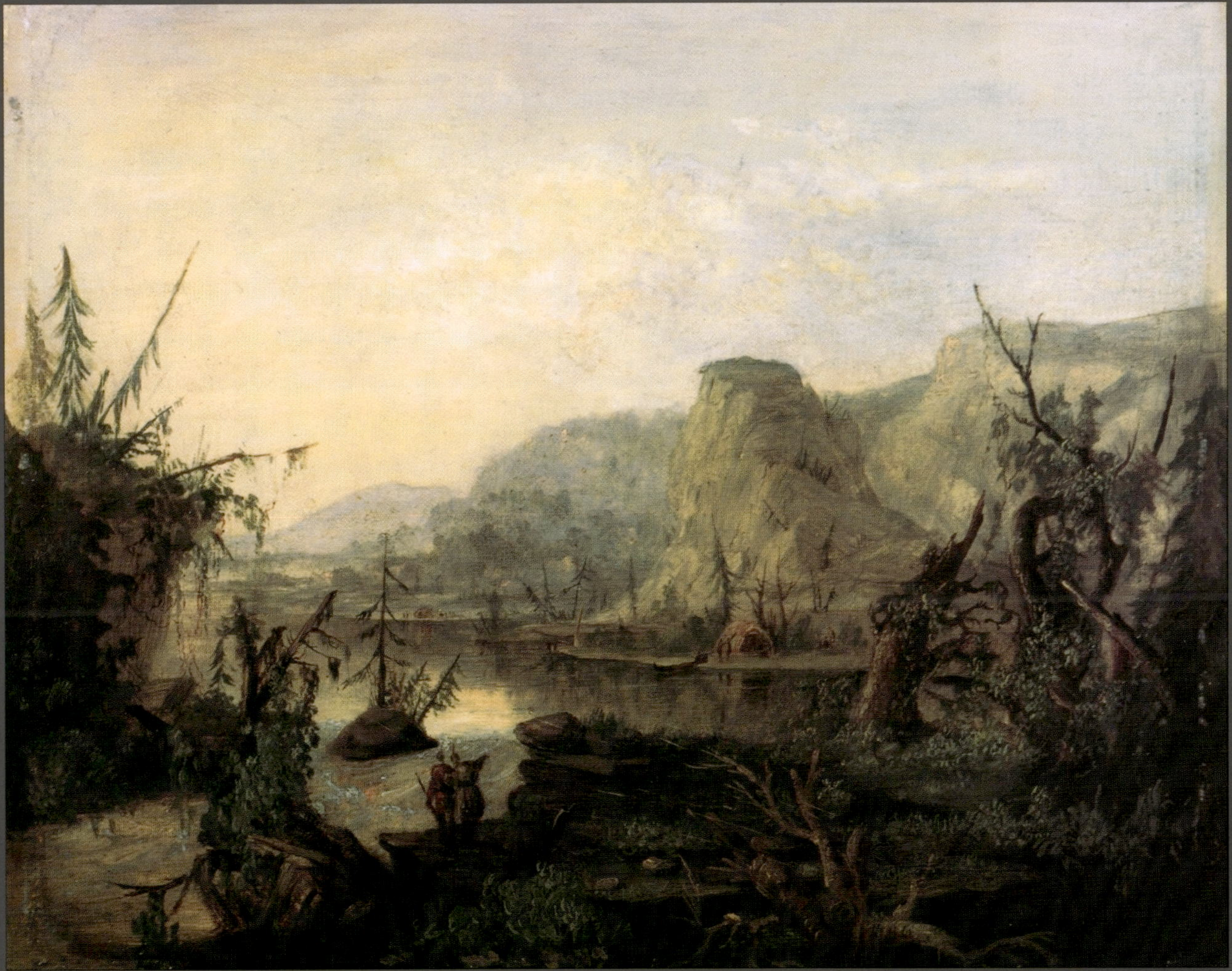

Fig. 5. Robert S. Duncanson, *Carp River, Lake Superior,* 1850, oil on canvas, 8 × 10 inches. Private Collection.

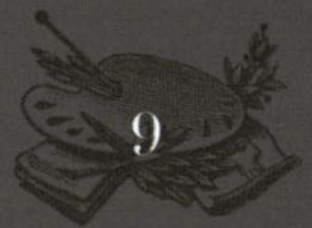

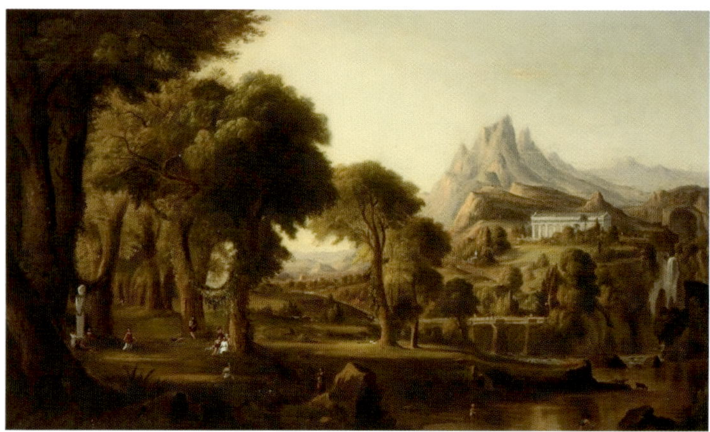

Fig. 6. Robert S. Duncanson, *Dream of Arcadia*, 1852, oil on canvas, 24 × 42 inches. Private Collection, Charles Kaufman Photography.

murals to decorate the foyer of Nicholas Longworth's stately home, Belmont [c.1850-52, Fig. 10].

The success of these ambitious commissions from abolitionist sympathizers earned the artist a sponsor, possibly Longworth, to pay for the traditional artistic pilgrimage across Europe known as the "grand tour." Duncanson departed in 1853 with his friend and colleague William Sonntag and traveled through England, France, and Italy to "finish" his art education. Duncanson responded to European art with self-confidence. During his travels, the artist discovered a direction for his career and he issued himself a personal challenge, "Every day that brakes [sic], to my vision, sheds a new light over my path—what was once dark and misty is gradually becoming brighter.

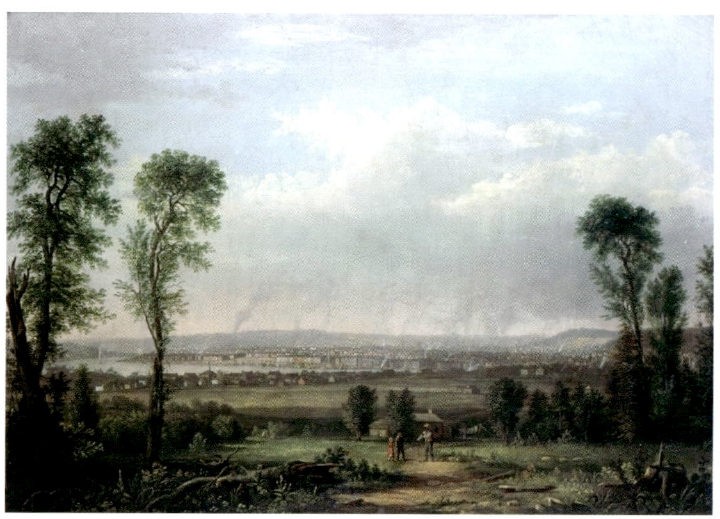

Fig. 7. Robert S. Duncanson, *View of Cincinnati, Ohio from Covington, Kentucky*, c. 1851, oil on canvas, 25 × 36 inches. Cincinnati Museum Center — Cincinnati Historical Society Library, Ohio.

My trip to Europe has to some extent enabled me to judge of my own talent. Of all the landscapes I saw in Europe, (and I saw thousands) I do not feel discouraged.... Someday I will return."[17] What Duncanson saw in Europe was a tradition of academic painting that advocated historical, biblical, and mythological subjects as the highest form of artistic expression. In the United States, Durand and the National Academy of Design expanded this concept to include landscape painting, with the most important eliciting "the profound and elevated emotions which the contemplation of the visible works of God awaken."[18]

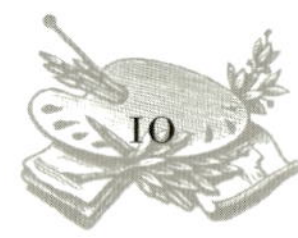

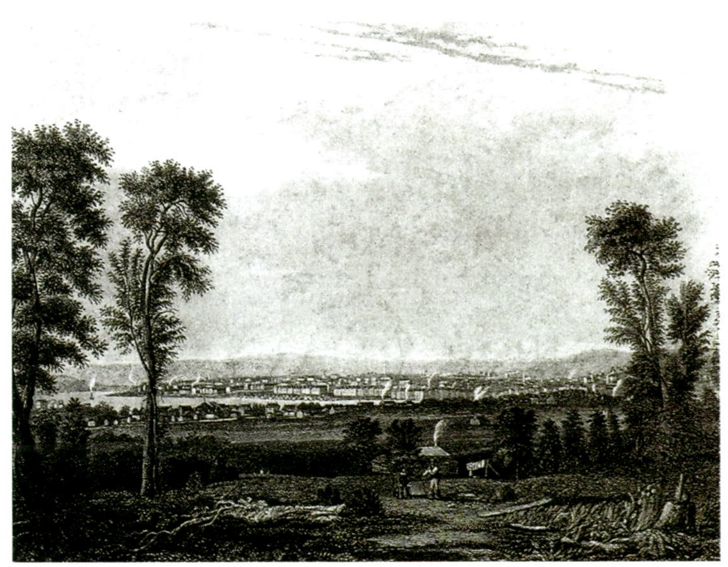

Fig. 8. J. W. Steel, *View of Cincinnati, Ohio from Covington, Kentucky*, from an original daguerreotype in *Graham's Magazine* 32 no. 6, 1848, p. 352.

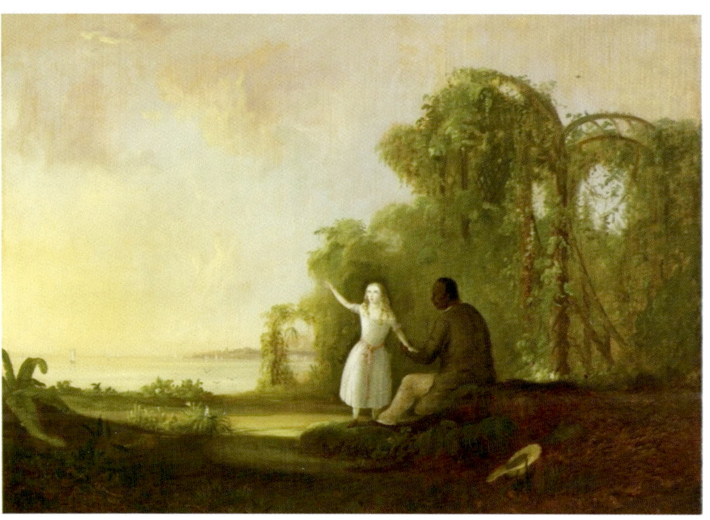

Fig. 9. Robert S. Duncanson, *Uncle Tom and Little Eva*, 1853, oil on canvas, 27 ¼ × 38 ¼ inches. Detroit Institute of Arts, gift of Mrs. Jefferson Butler and Miss Grace Conover/The Bridgeman Art Library, New York, New York.

For many American landscape painters, and now for Duncanson as well, this meant a "great picture" with a didactic, moralizing subject, often taken from literature. Duncanson vowed that, once he had created his "masterpiece," he would return to Europe to exhibit with the pantheon of Europe's great artists.

Duncanson, like many Americans, was fascinated by Italy and its ancient ruins that resonated with metaphors for the decay of civilizations. Thomas Cole had introduced the subject of Italian ruins to the vocabulary of American landscape painting. Once again, Duncanson followed Cole's example and upon his return from his "grand tour" created a series of ambitious views of ancient ruins including *Time's Temple* [1854, Fig. 11]. With this, his largest easel painting to date, Duncanson hoped to create a major artistic statement of his technical accomplishments, applying the lessons learned on his grand tour for his American audience. Cole had articulated the concept of the cycle of civilizations in an essay published a decade earlier, "Our only means

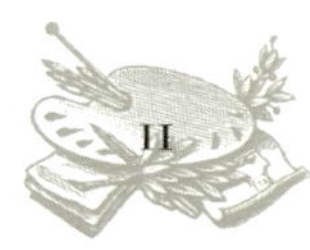

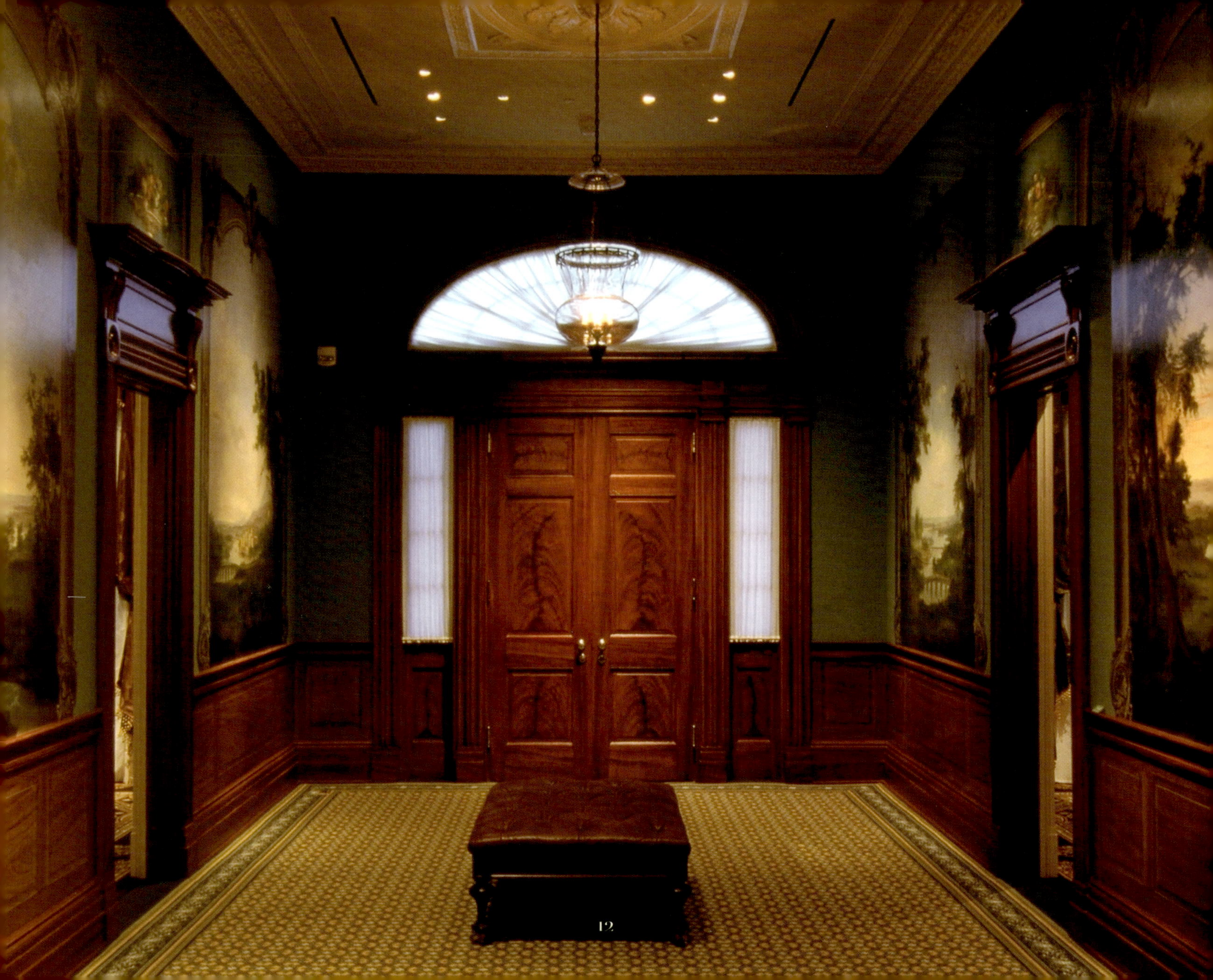

of judging the future is the past. We see that nations have sprung from obscurity, risen to glory, and decayed. Their rise has in general been marked by virtue; their decadence by vice, vanity, and licentiousness. Let us beware."[19] In his own morality lesson, Duncanson was also likely to be sensitive to the "vice" of slavery practiced by the Romans and its moral associations for his contemporaries as a cautionary tale of their own possible fate. Throughout the remainder of his career Duncanson created scenes of romantic ruins, including *The Temple of the Sibyl* [1859, Fig. 12], which he created in direct competition with his former colleague William Sonntag's painting, *Italian Lake with Classical Ruins* (1858, Hood Museum of Art, Dartmouth College).

The 1850s witnessed the height of the Abolitionist movement. At this time Cincinnati became a hotbed of the anti-slavery movement and a population center for "free colored persons." Duncanson responded to Frederick Douglass's call to "strike for the freedom of the slave, and for the rights of human nature,"and participated in abolitionist societies. On several occasions he donated paintings to benefit anti-slavery activities. Notices of his work regularly appeared in the anti-slavery journals of the day, which reported his life story, his exhibitions, and his contributions to African-American society. Most significantly, he collaborated with his friend and neighbor James Pressley Ball (1825-1905?), an African-American daguerrean, on an anti-slavery panorama, *Ball's Splendid Mammoth Pictorial Tour of the United States* [1855, Fig. 14].

Capitalizing on the popularity of scenic Mississippi River panoramas, Ball and Duncanson created a 600-yard-wide panorama to portray the horrors of human bondage, which toured the United States for several years. Presented in theaters, the panorama unfurled as the audience listened to a narration with sound and lighting effects. The narrator guided spectators through the slave trade, beginning with capture in Africa, the transcontinental passage, slave markets, and escape up the Mississippi to freedom in Canada. Although the panorama itself is lost, the surviving script confirms Ball's intention to condemn American hypocrisy as "the land of the free, and the home of the *slave*."[20] Ball modeled his panorama on two from 1850 based on the slave narratives of Henry Box Brown and William Wells Brown.[21] However, Ball distinguished his panorama from the former by advertising that it was "painted by Negroes." This certainly refers to Duncanson, the principal artist working in Ball's Gallery at this time, and his large staff, which included several African Americans who listed themselves in the census as "artists" or "daguerreans."[22]

Although Duncanson primarily painted landscapes after 1848, he still executed portraits of abolitionist leaders and sympathizers upon commission. The roster of his sitters reads like the lexicon of the anti-slavery movement in Cincinnati including James Birney (c. 1855, location unknown), Robert Bishop (c.1855, location unknown), Freeman C. Cary (c. 1855, Smithsonian American Art Museum), Nicholas Longworth (1858, University of Cincinnati), and Richard S. Rust I

Fig. 10. Entry foyer of the Baum-Taft House with murals by Robert S. Duncanson, bequest of Mr. and Mrs. Charles Phelps Taft, Cincinnati, Ohio. Tony Walsh Photography.

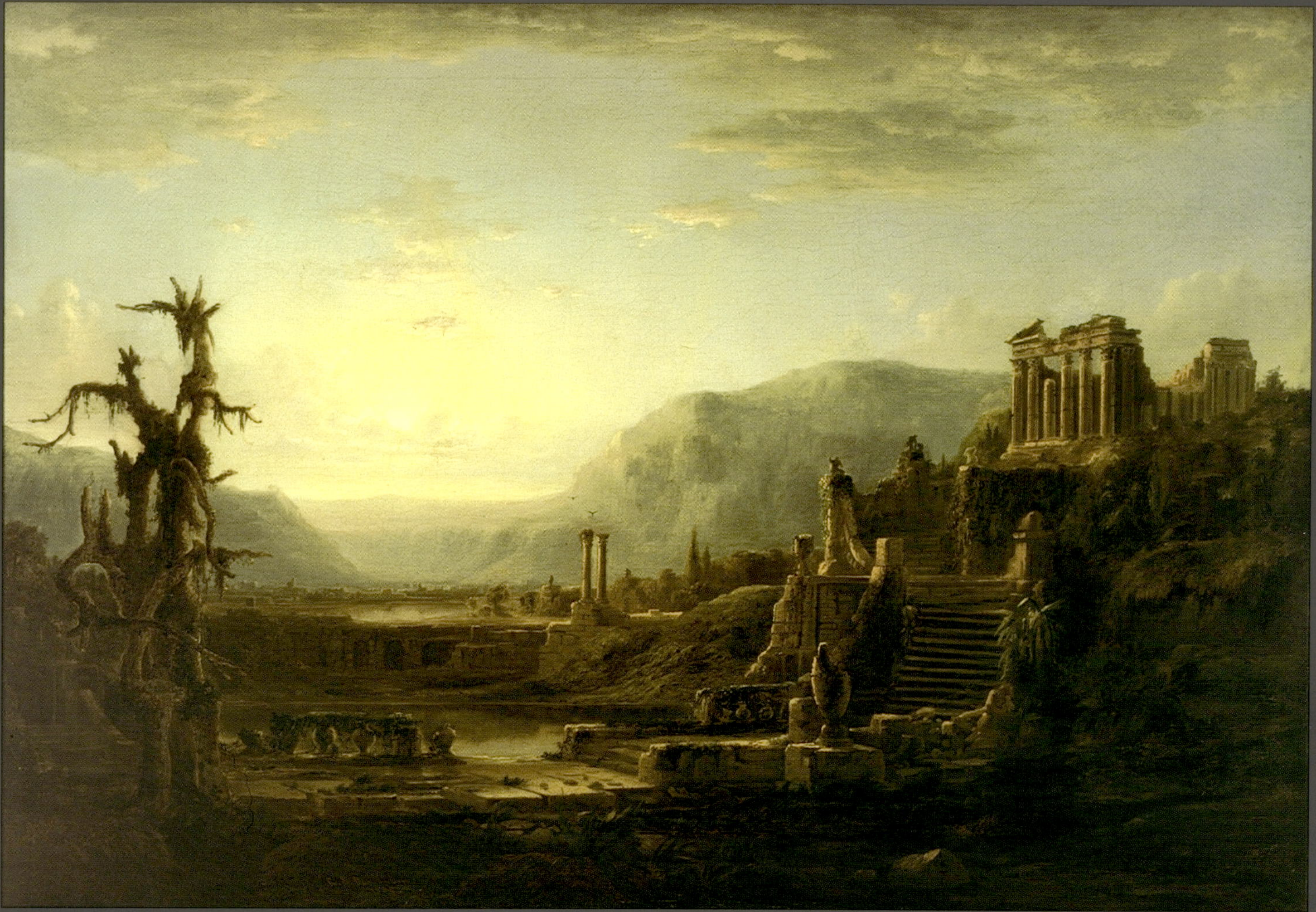

Fig. 11. Robert S. Duncanson, *Time's Temple*, 1854, oil on canvas, 34 × 59 inches. Howard University Gallery of Art, Washington, DC.

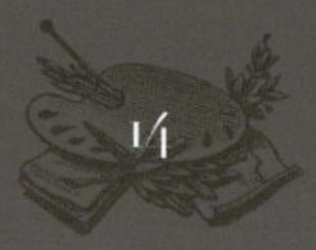

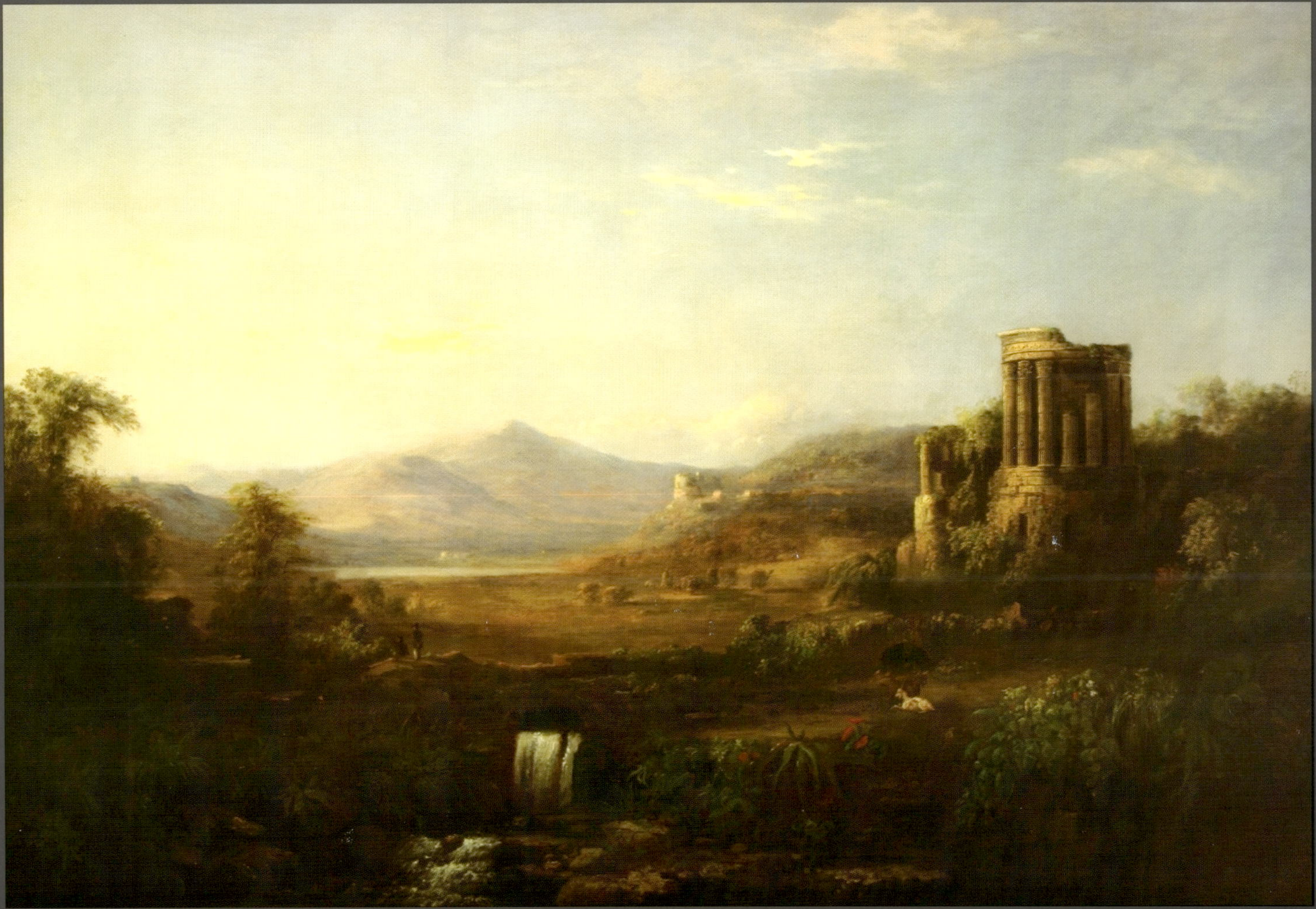

Fig. 12. Robert S. Duncanson, *The Temple of the Sibyl*, 1859, oil on canvas, 35 × 50 inches. Springfield Museum of Art, Ohio.

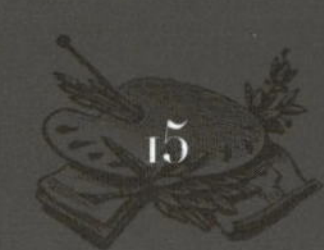

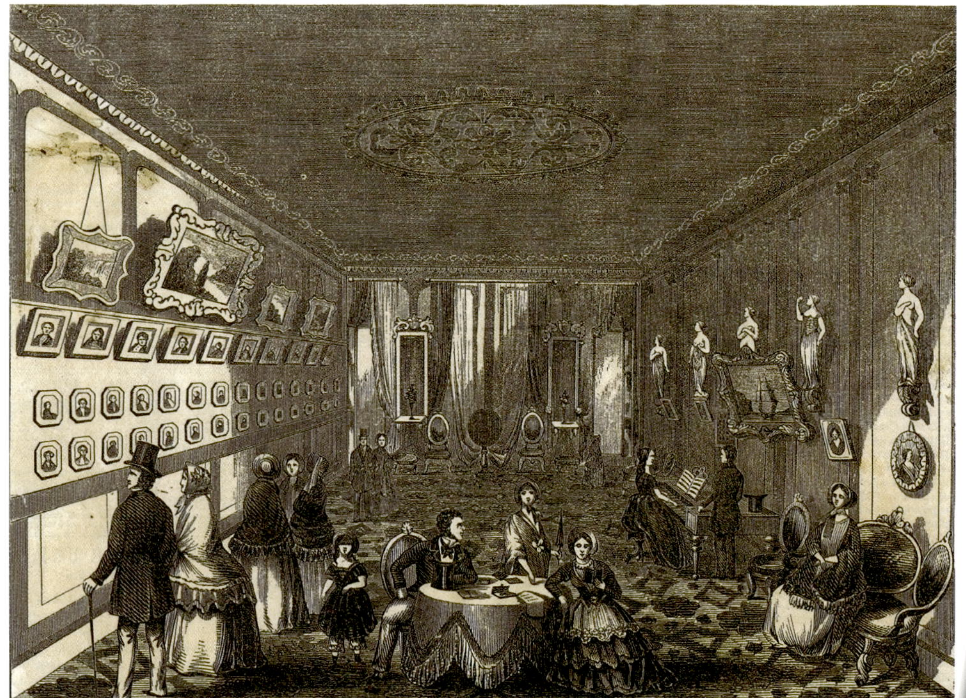

Fig. 13. *Ball's Daguerrean Gallery*, 1855, engraving, in J. Pressley Ball's Splendid Mammoth Pictorial Tour of the United States. 1855. Cincinnati Museum Center — Cincinnati Historical Society Library, Ohio.

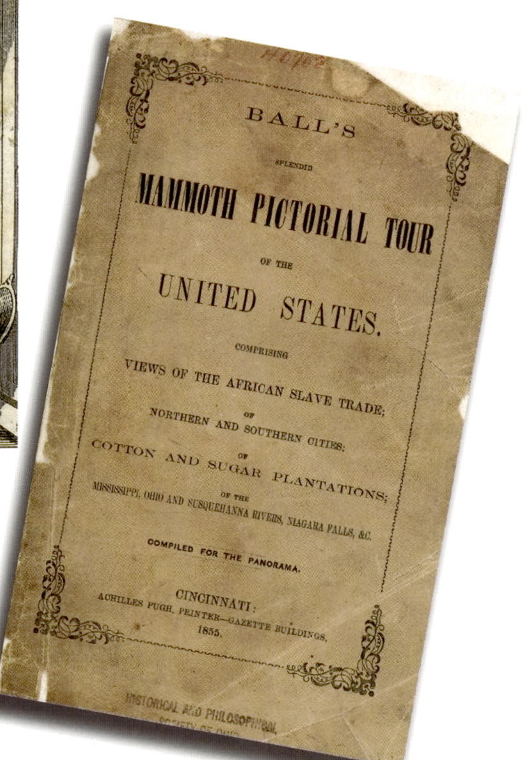

BALL'S

SPLENDID

MAMMOTH PICTORIAL TOUR

OF THE

UNITED STATES.

COMPRISING

VIEWS OF THE AFRICAN SLAVE TRADE;

OF

NORTHERN AND SOUTHERN CITIES;

OF

COTTON AND SUGAR PLANTATIONS;

OF THE

MISSISSIPPI, OHIO AND SUSQUEHANNA RIVERS, NIAGARA FALLS, &C.

COMPILED FOR THE PANORAMA.

CINCINNATI:

ACHILLES PUGH, PRINTER—GAZETTE BUILDINGS,

1855.

Fig. 14. *Ball's Splendid Mammoth Pictorial Tour of the United States. Comprising Views of the African Slave Trade, of Northern and Southern Cities, of Cotton and Sugar Plantations of the Mississippi, Ohio and Susquehanna Rivers, Niagara Falls, &c. Cincinnati*: Achilles Pugh, Printer, 1855. Cincinnati Museum Center — Cincinnati Historical Society Library, Ohio.

[1858, Fig. 15]. These paintings confirm Duncanson's close connection to the abolitionist movement in his community. Rust's portrait commemorates his appointment in 1858 as the first president of Wilberforce College, a school established for African Americans. He was known to have hosted weekly dinners attended by the region's educators, abolitionists, and family friends. It appears quite likely that Duncanson was present at these soirees, judging by this portrait and the number of his landscape paintings that were passed down through generations of the Rust family.

By the end of the 1850s, fear of an imminent civil conflict dominated the American political scene. Congress could not resolve the disputes over slavery and states rights, and public opinion on these subjects reached a fever pitch. Duncanson responded by creating a series of literary-historical paintings that reflect his thoughts on the quickly degenerating political situation. As early as 1854, immediately after his return from his "grand tour," Duncanson stated his ambition "to create a great picture"[23] that he would exhibit on his return to Europe. The looming crisis provided a subject of personal significance and grave political implications. The artist started his ambitious *Land of the Lotos Eaters* [1861, Fig. 16] in December of 1860 when the Civil War seemed imminent and completed the work for public exhibition as the Civil War began. The painting stands as Duncanson's futile appeal to the nation to resolve its differences.[24]

At this time Duncanson also created an extended group of allegorical figure paintings drawn from classical mythology and romantic literature. As a companion to his *Lotos Eaters* he painted an image of

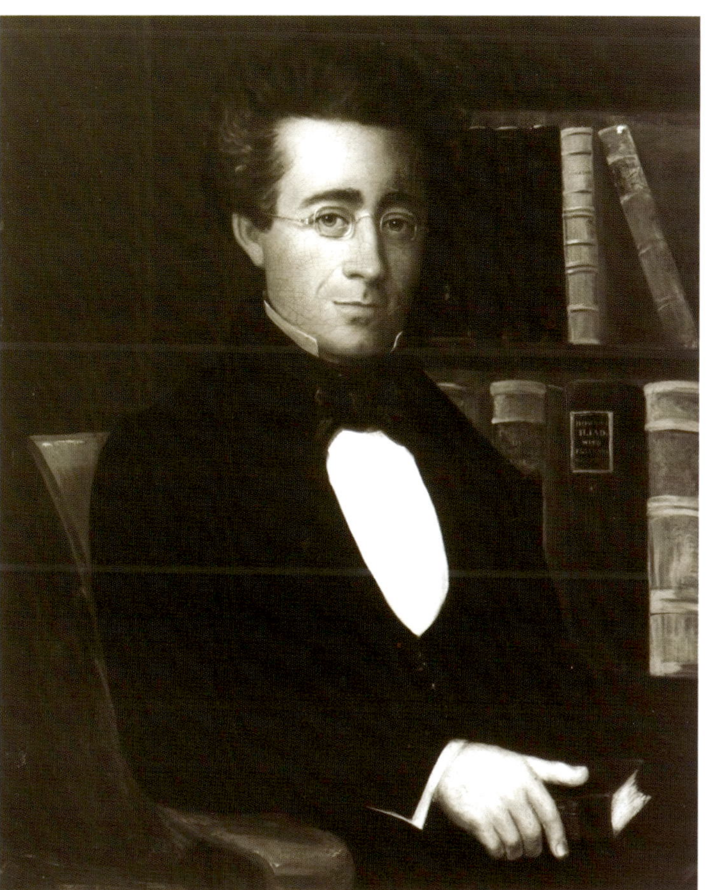

Fig. 15. Robert S. Duncanson. *Richard Sutton Rust I*, 1858, oil on canvas, 30 × 25 inches. Richard S. Rust IV, Cincinnati, Ohio.

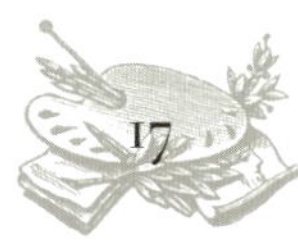

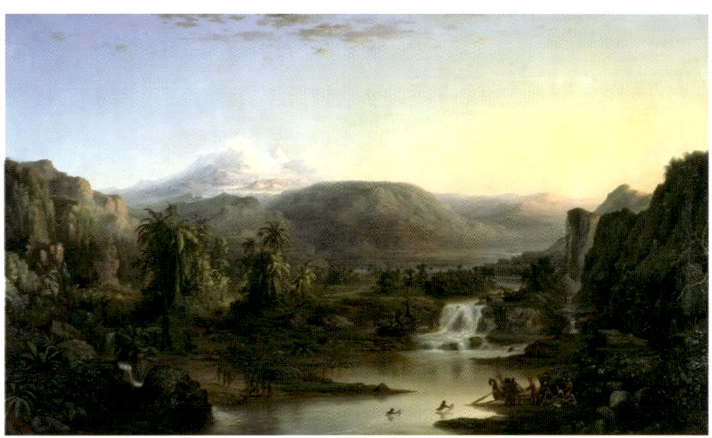

Fig. 16. Robert S. Duncanson, *Land of the Lotos Eaters*, 1861, oil on canvas, 52 ¾ × 88 ⅝ inches. The Royal Court Sweden. Alexis Daflos Photography.

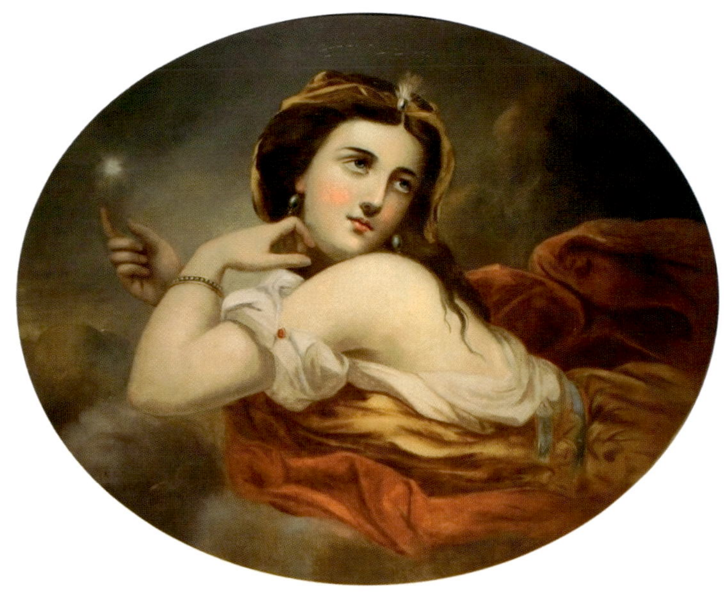

Fig. 17. Robert S. Duncanson, *Allegorical Figure*, 1860, oil on canvas, 28 ⅞ × 36 inches. Alexander Gallery, New York.

Oenone mourning her deceased children (location unknown). He also painted ambitious full-length figures of *Calliope* on commission for Wabash University (location unknown) and a *Faith* in 1862 (National Afro-American Museum and Cultural Center, Wilberforce, Ohio). The *Allegorical Figure* from 1860 is certainly his most accomplished figure painting [Fig. 17]. Although it is difficult to determine precisely the subject, it appears to be a Peri, a fallen angel who has been redeemed, from Thomas Moore's epic poem *Lalla Rookh* (1817), one of Duncanson's favorite literary sources. *Lalla Rookh* was one of the most popular poems of its day, capitalizing on the Euro-American fascination with oriental subjects. The story revolves around four epic poems that were recited to Lalla Rookh by her escort during her journey to Kashmir to marry the King of Lesser Bucharia. The tale of "Paradise and the Peri" relates the repeated attempts of a fallen angel to gain admittance to heaven. On the third attempt, the Peri, a "child of air," presents to God a tear from the cheek of a repentant, evil man, and gains her salvation.[25] The figure floating across the clouds with her flowing robes held by the clasp on her veil, could well represent the artist's vision of the Peri.

Duncanson had planned to exhibit his *Land of the Lotos Eaters* across the United States and Europe. However, the outbreak of the Civil War disrupted his plans. Cincinnati, on the border of the Confederacy, experienced great political turmoil and increased racial tension during this time. According to the *Cincinnati Weekly Gazette*, "The war in the South, the fear of being arrested for endeavoring to evade the draft, and many other considerations consequent on the war, have prevented [artists] from traveling so much as usual."[26] In lieu of summer sketching expeditions, Cincinnati artists reactivated the Cincinnati Sketch Club, which found renewed purpose during the Civil War. The Club met bimonthly for members to share with one another the sketches they created on a predetermined literary subject. For the March 1863 meeting, the Club members produced sketches inspired by Moore's *Lalla Rookh* (1817). An article appeared in the *Cincinnati Daily Enquirer* on this session of the Sketch Club remarking on the large number of sketches submitted, including one by Duncanson [Fig. 18]. The final poem, "The Light of the Haram," is the source for Duncanson's painting, depicting the lush scenery in the Vale of Kashmir. This epic poem fascinated Duncanson, who painted four versions of it through the 1860s, making it the largest series the artist devoted to a single literary source. Over the development of his series, Duncanson increasingly amplified the exotic tropical setting and architecture, culminating in the final *Vale of Kashmir* [1870, Fig. 19], with shooting fountains, tall palm trees, and exotic palaces.

During the summer of 1862, Duncanson traveled north away from the conflict, up the Mississippi River into Canada, where he could sketch more freely and, simultaneously, investigate the possibility of emigrating. The resulting paintings depict some of the region's scenic landmarks including *Minnehaha Falls* [1862, Fig. 20], made famous by Henry Wadsworth Longfellow's *Song of Hiawatha*. Published only a few years earlier in 1855, Longfellow's poem became instantly popular, particularly with artists, as an "American" epic that ennobled Native Americans.[27] Referencing his literary source, Duncanson places an Indian woman, possibly Minnehaha herself, at the foot of the falls for which she was named, hearing the voices of her ancestors.

Native Americans became a *leit motif* for Duncanson, a subject that appears repeatedly throughout his career and appears to have carried deep personal associations for the artist. Duncanson also painted two views of *Minnenopa Falls* [1862, Fig. 21] (properly spelled *Minneopa*), a scenic falls in southern Minnesota, that the artist ties to Longfellow by painting a male Indian in a position similar to Minnehaha's, viewing and listening to the falls. Although Minneopa does not appear in Longfellow, Duncanson is clearly referencing the poem and capitalizing on its popularity. His choice of *The Song of Hiawatha* for these two series may not be purely literary. One scholar has proposed that minority artists have often "appropriated a literary theme from an 'empowered' author whose text positively affirms the artist's racial, ethnic, and/or religious difference."[28] African Americans of this era commonly empathized with the plight of a similarly disenfranchised ethnic group, a sentiment manifest in Duncanson's many depictions of Indians. As early as

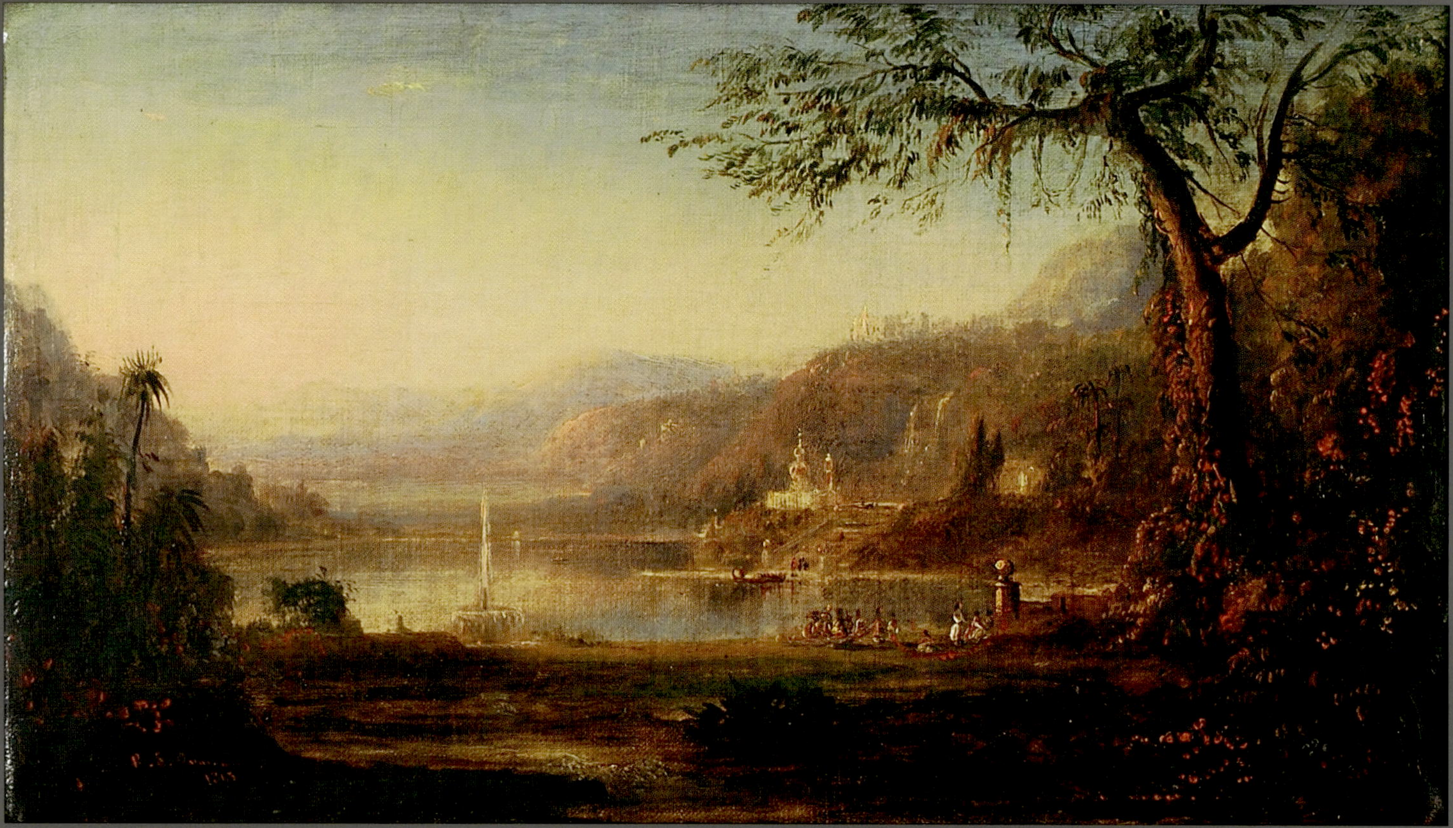

Fig. 18. Robert S. Duncanson, *Vale of Kashmir*, 1863, oil on canvas, 9 × 16 inches. David Hausrath, Fort Thomas, Kentucky.

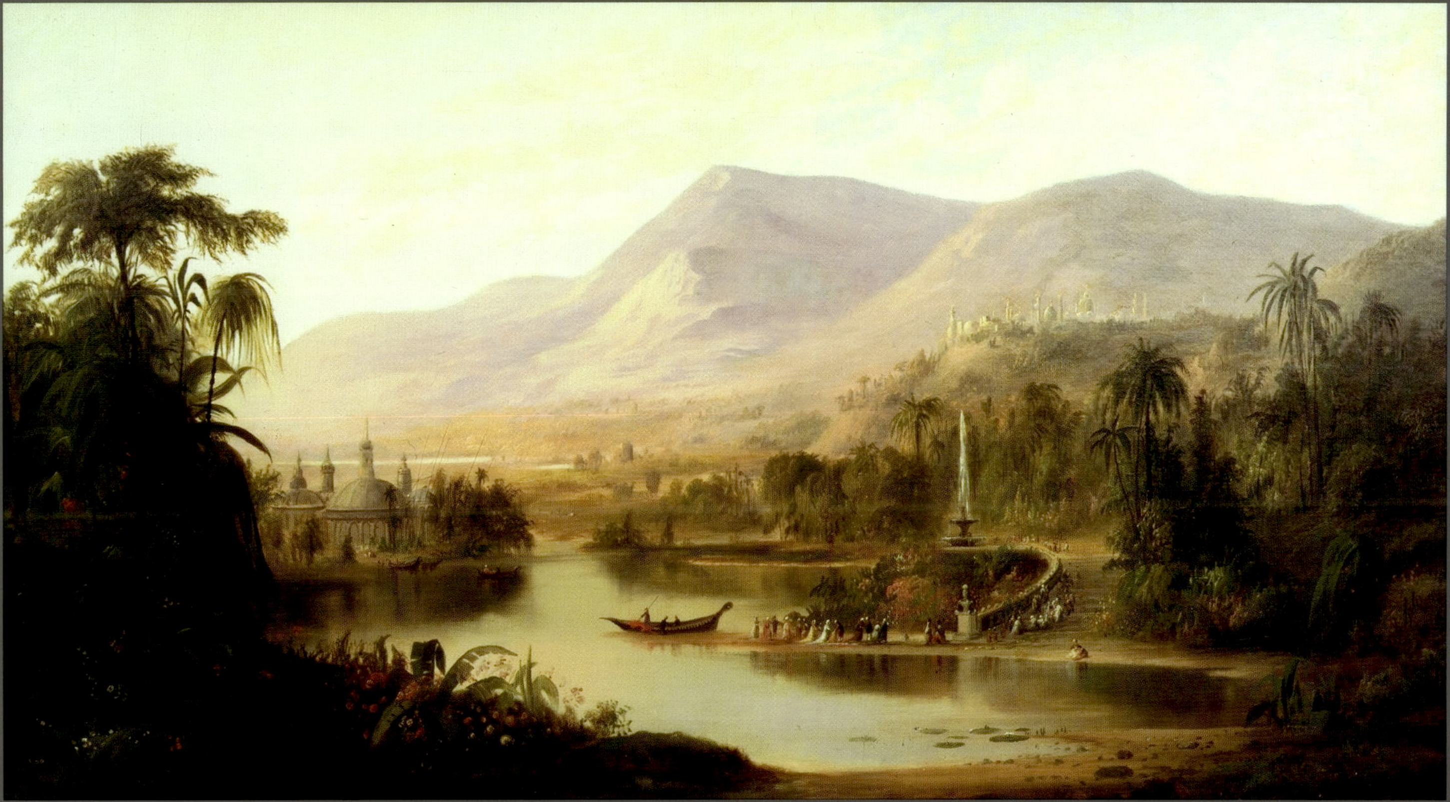

Fig. 19. Robert S. Duncanson, *Vale of Kashmir*, 1870, oil on canvas, 26 × 49 ¼ inches. George Wein, New York, New York; Courtesy of Michael Rosenfeld Galley, LLC, New York, New York.

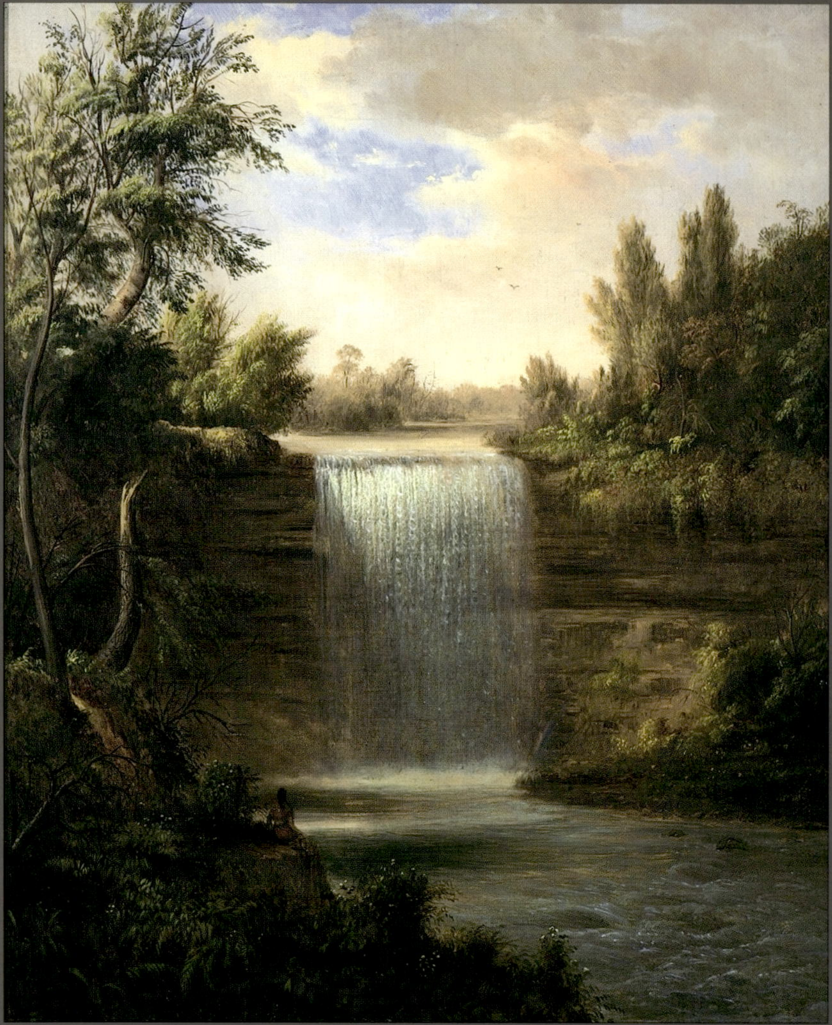

Fig. 20. Robert S. Duncanson, *Minnehaha Falls*, 1862, oil on canvas, 20 × 16 inches. Howard University Gallery of Art, Washington, DC.

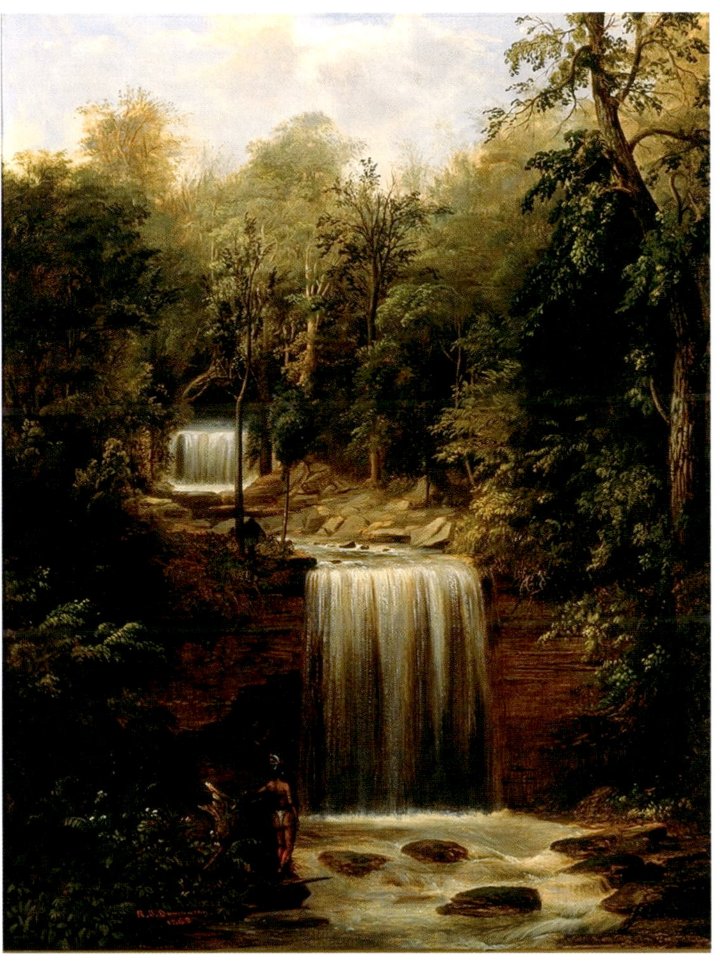

1846 in *Hunting in the Woods* [Fig. 22], the artist portrays a Native American striding freely through the forest in pursuit of his prey. In *Western Landscape* [1861, Fig. 23], Duncanson situates an Indian lodge in the middle ground with what may be Native Americans standing outside. Even in his copy of Frederic E. Church's *Heart of the Andes* from 1871 (Kalamazoo Museum of Art, Michigan), he includes a battle scene between an Indian and American soldiers that has no relationship to Church, but certainly has great personal significance to the artist. The preponderance of evidence suggests that Duncanson utilized the Native American as a parallel, or even an alter ego, to his own African-American identity.

By the summer of 1863 the prospects for peace were remote, and the bleak situation forced Duncanson into self-imposed exile. Escaping the war, he intended to emigrate to England with his "great pictures." However, as an African American, he could not obtain a passport, so he fled to Canada where he could easily leave for England. In September 1863, Duncanson arrived in Montreal where a journalist reported, "his color did not prevent his association with other artists and his entrance into good society."[29] Canada warmly welcomed the distinguished American landscape painter, where he received effusive praise for his famous *Lotos Eaters*. During his years there, the Canadian landscape captivated Duncanson's imagination. He painted extraordinary romantic scenes such as *Mt. Orford* [1864, Fig. 24], which

Fig. 21. Robert S. Duncanson, *Minnenopa Falls*, 1862, oil on canvas, 20 × 16 inches. Milwaukee Art Museum, Purchase, Andrew A. Ziegler Fund M2007.37. John R. Glembin Photography.

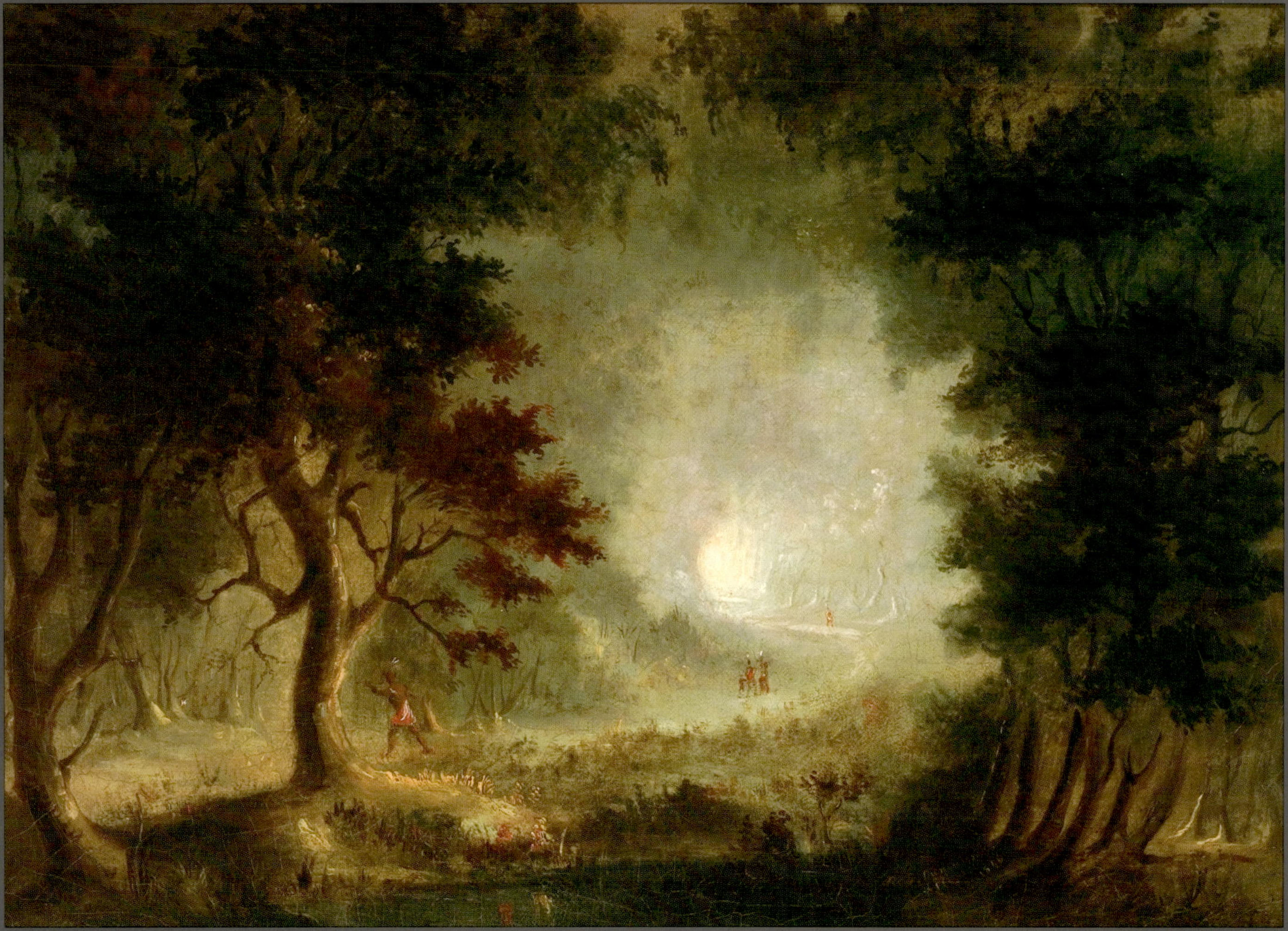

Fig. 22. Robert S. Duncanson, *Hunting in the Woods*, 1846, oil on canvas, 12 ¾ × 18 ½ inches. Dr. Dianne Whitfield-Locke, Mitchellville, Maryland.

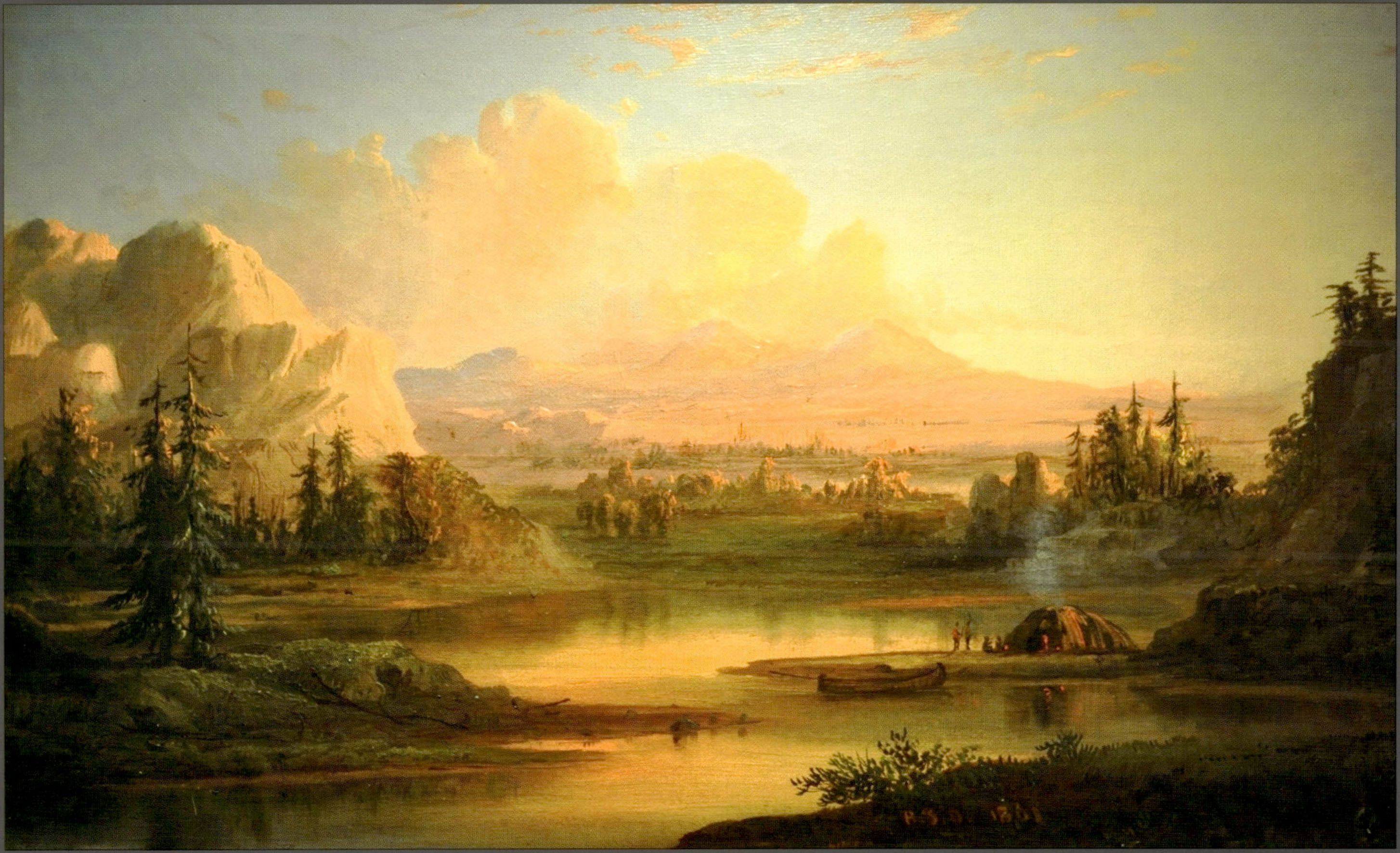

Fig. 23. Robert S. Duncanson, *Western Landscape*, 1861, oil on canvas, 9 × 15 inches. Private Collection.

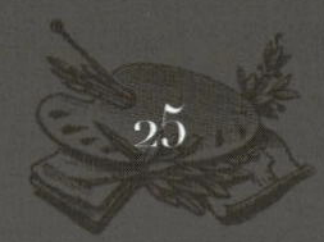

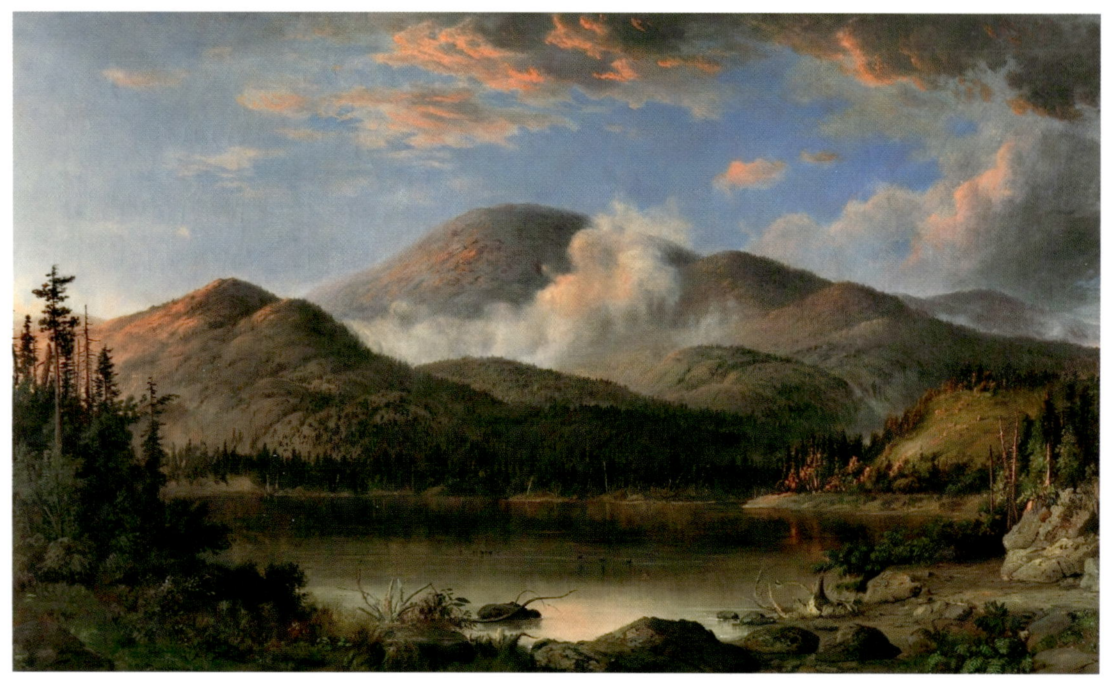

Fig. 24. Robert S. Duncanson, *Mt. Orford*, 1864, oil on canvas, 31 × 52 inches. Babcock Gallery, New York, New York.

features this natural landmark on Lake Memphremagog. Duncanson intended to only pass through Canada on his way to England; however, he remained for two years and was rewarded with a respect that he was unaccustomed to as an African American in the United States. Prior to his arrival, Canadian artists had little exposure to Hudson River style painting. But largely due to Duncanson's influence, Canadians witnessed the development of a national school of landscape painting. Interestingly, Duncanson's race was never cited in any of the articles, correspondence, or references to him during his years in Canada, while in the United States the specter of his racial heritage always loomed.

In 1865 Duncanson finally departed for the British Isles, traveling with two Canadian artists, his pupil Allan Edson, and CJ Way. In Dublin, Duncanson exhibited his *Lotos Eaters* at the International Exposition as a Canadian in the Canadian pavilion. However, it was in London that Duncanson achieved his greatest ambition when a critic

for the prestigious *London Art Journal* proclaimed that the *Lotos Eaters* was "wrought with the skill of a master."[30] In England, Duncanson was avidly patronized by the aristocracy, who recognized him as one of the important American landscape painters of the day. Motivated by the novels of Sir Walter Scott, Duncanson also toured the picturesque Scottish Highlands. The land and lore of Scotland enchanted the painter, resulting in a series of rugged landscapes, such as the *Scottish Landscape* [Fig. 25], that he painted up to the end of his career. Interestingly, Scott's English romantic literature held great significance for many contemporary African Americans. When Frederick Douglass abandoned his slave name, he adopted his surname, Douglass, from the name of the rebel Highland lord in Scott's poem, *The Lady of the Lake* (1810). And, W.E.B. Du Bois fondly remembered Scott's poem from his youth and referred to it as the "sort of world we want to create for ourselves and all in America."[31] In essence, Duncanson's *Scottish Landscape* represents the paradise on earth that he and other African Americans sought.

Surprisingly, after having achieved his career goal, the artist stayed in England for only one year. By the winter of 1866-67, Duncanson was back in Cincinnati exhibiting his new Scottish landscapes with the confidence of an artist who had realized his ambition. Tragically, at this time, Duncanson began to suffer from dementia that led to violent outbursts, delusions, and hallucinations. In fact, his condition may account for his short stay in England. By 1870 the artist believed that he was possessed by the spirit of a deceased female artist, who assisted him in the creation of his paintings. In October 1872, while installing an exhibition of his work in Detroit, he suffered a seizure and collapsed. He was taken to a local sanatorium, where he died on December 21, 1872.

In the mid-nineteenth century Duncanson became one of the leading landscape painters in North America. This would be a remarkable achievement under any circumstances, but it is even more remarkable in light of the obstacles he faced. Duncanson assimilated into the Anglo-European art community to a degree that was unprecedented among African Americans. He actively participated in the Euro-American art community, creating paintings that glorified nature while employing the natural and literary metaphors of his day. Through his subtle strategy of inserting slaves and Native Americans into his paintings and through his rendering of historical and literary subjects, he elevated his landscapes into tableaus that were ripe with meaning for both Anglo-American and African-American viewers. His art reflects the two cultures that influenced his life: the European American and the African American. During his career he made tremendous strides toward diversifying art in North America, making substantive contributions to the cultural histories of both Canada and the United States. Duncanson's life and work exemplify Du Bois's conception of an African American who recognizes his "double consciousness" and, "simply wishes to make it possible for a man to be both a Negro and an American, without being cursed and spit upon by his fellows, without having the doors of Opportunity closed roughly in his face."[32] Indeed, Duncanson embodies this model. Although it is not immediately obvious, a close reading of some of his paintings

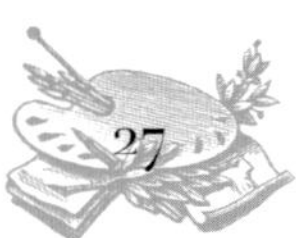

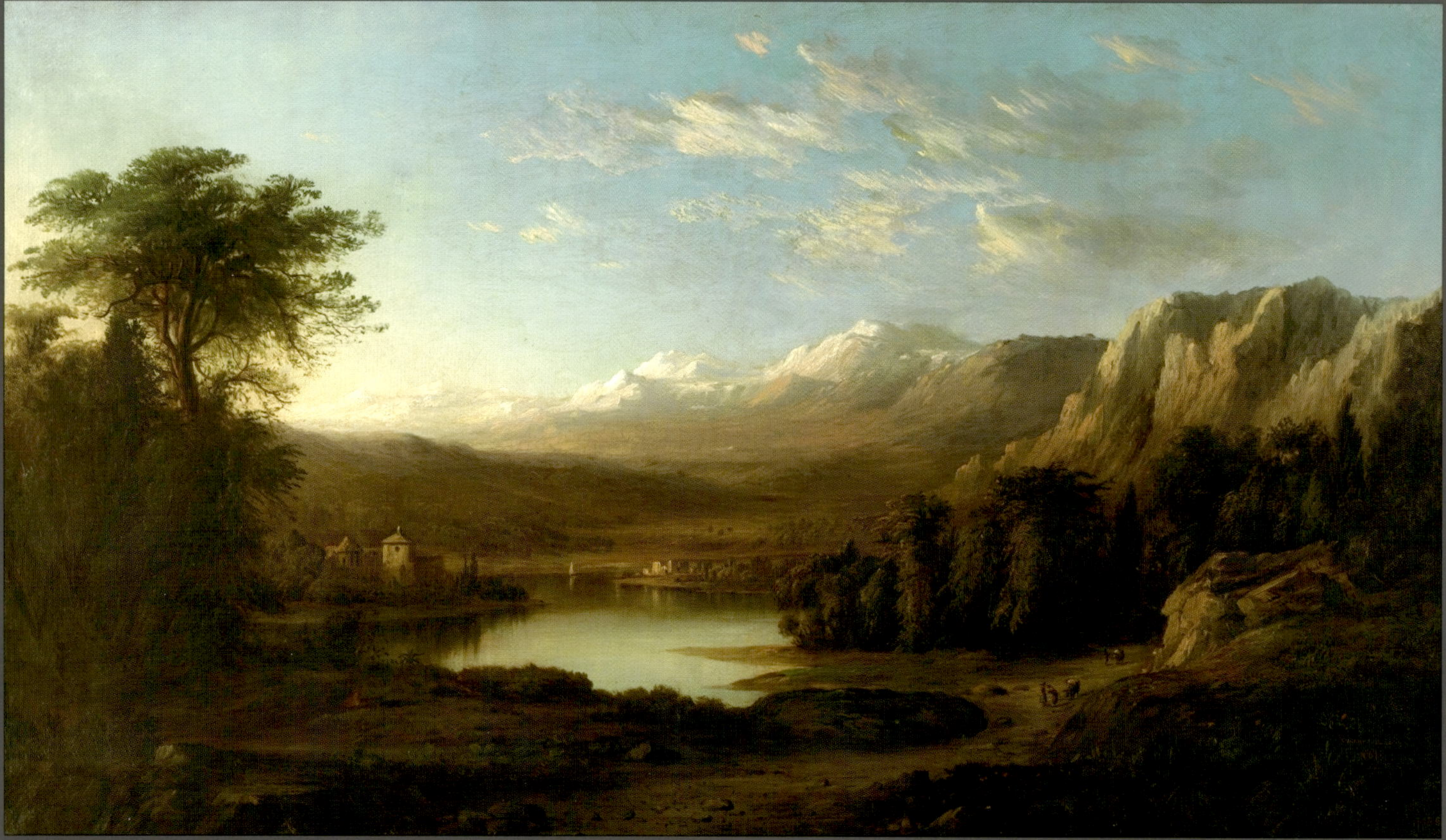

Fig. 25. Robert S. Duncanson, *Scottish Landscape*, 1871, oil on canvas, 20 × 36 inches. William Rybolt, Cincinnati, Ohio.

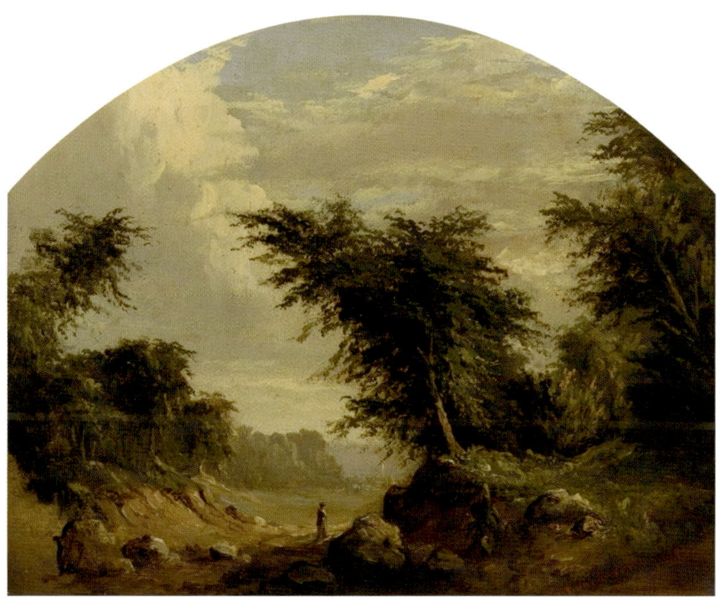

Fig. 26. Robert S. Duncanson, *Untitled* (Landscape), c. 1860-65. oil on board, 7 ½ × 9 ½ inches. Dr. Ronald & Mrs. Patricia Walters, Silver Spring, Maryland.

in the context of the political and social circumstances that shaped the artist's life, signify the African-American perspective in his art and endow his paintings with complex nuances of meaning that make them enriching experiences. The grandson of a freedman, Duncanson's artistic ambitions and the content of his paintings epitomize Du Bois' statement that "the spiritual striving of the freedmen's sons is the travail of souls." [33]

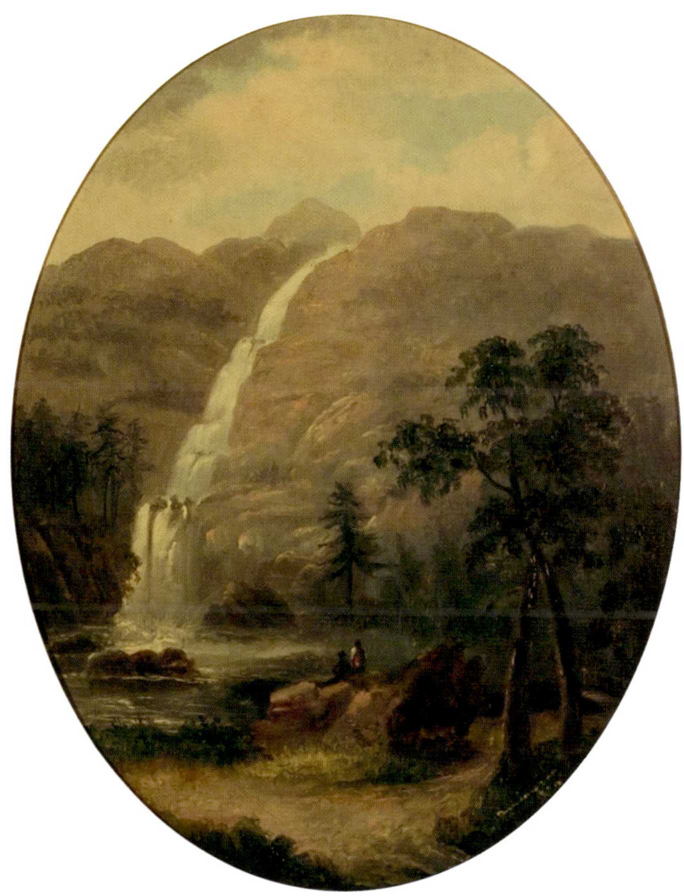

Fig. 27. Robert S. Duncanson, *Mountain Pool*, 1870, oil on board, 14 × 11 inches, Kenkeleba House, New York, New York.

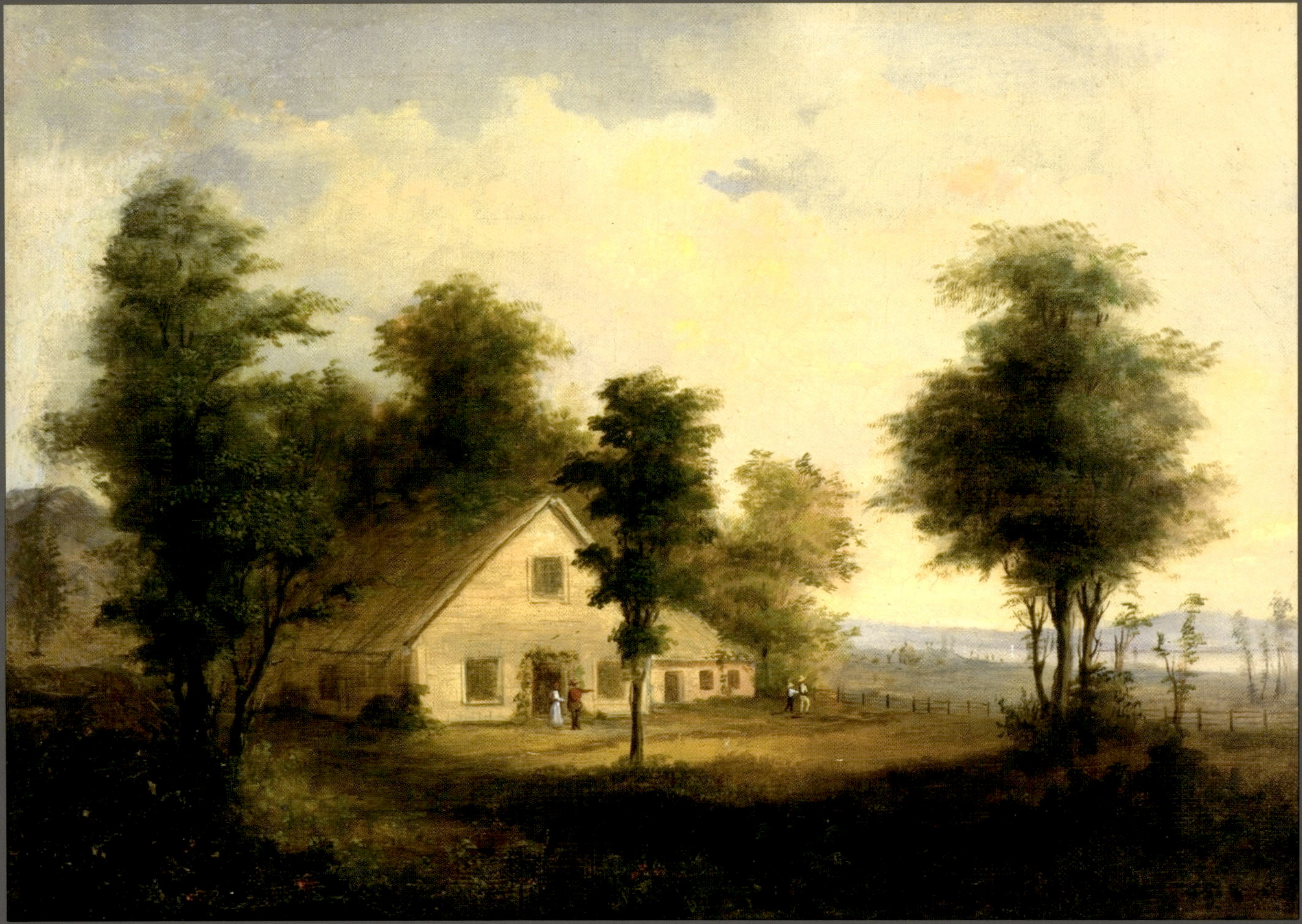

Fig. 28. Robert S. Duncanson, *Summer*, 1849, oil on canvas, 11 ½ × 16 ⅜ inches. Michael Rosenfeld Gallery, LLC, New York, New York.

Endnotes

1 Du Bois, W.E.B. *The Souls of Black Folk*. First edition 1903, London and New York: Penguin Publishers, 1989, pp. 12.

2 Asher B. Durand, "Letters on Landscape Painting, VIII," *The Crayon* 1, no. 23 (June 6, 1855), p. 369.

3 *Daily Cincinnati Gazette* (May 30, 1861), p. 3.

4 "Art Association Conversazione," *Montreal Herald* (February 12, 1864), p. 2.

5 "*The Land of the Lotos-Eaters*. Painted by R.S. Duncanson," *Art-Journal* (London), n.s., v. 5 (1866), p. 93.

6 Since the 1980s revision of American Art history, numbers of art historians dealing with American landscape painting have read cultural identity into the landscape paintings of this era beginning with Barbara Novak's *Nature and Culture: American Landscape and Painting*, 1825-1875 (New York: Oxford University Press, 1980), and continuing with such publications as Bryan Jay Wolf's *Romantic Re-Vision: Culture and Consciousness in Nineteenth-Century American Painting and Literature* (Chicago and London: The University of Chicago Press, 1982), William H. Truettner, ed., *The West as America: Reinterpreting Images of the Frontier, 1820-1920* (Washington and London: Smithsonian Institution Press, 1991), Angela Miller, *The Empire of the Eye: Landscape Representation and American Cultural Politics, 1925-1875* (Ithaca and London: Cornell University Press, 1993), and William H. Truettner and Alan Wallach, *Thomas Cole: Landscape into History* (New Haven and London: Yale University Press, 1994).

7 Du Bois, W.E.B. , *op. cit.*, pp. 5. See also Henry Louis Gates, Jr., *The Signifying Monkey* (New York and Oxford: Oxford University Press, 1988).

8 The discovery was made by Dennis Au, then curator of the Monroe County Historical Museum (Michigan), and reported in "Famous 19th century black artist's ties with Monroe are sketchy thus far," *Monroe Evening News* (27 March 1982).

9 Ira Berlin. *Slaves without Masters: The Free Negro in the Antebellum South*. New York: Pantheon Books, 1974; and V. Jacque Voegeli, *Free But Not Equal: The Midwest and the Negro During the Civil War*. Chicago: The University of Chicago Press, 1967.

10 See C.G. Woodson, "The Negroes of Cincinnati Prior to the Civil War," *The Journal of Negro History*, vol. 1, no. 1 (January 1916), pp. 1-22.

11 After surveying the US Census from the first census in 1790 to 1900, I tracked the Duncanson clan in every census beginning in 1820 until 1900, following their various moves from Fayette, New York, to Monroe, Michigan, to Cincinnati, Ohio, and finally Seattle, Washington. In every census all of the Duncansons, from the grandfather Charles, his son John Dean and his wife, Lucille, and their children, including Robert and his wife and children, are listed as mulatto. Duncanson's grandfather and his parents are recorded as being born in Virginia. This early biographical information was originally published in my book, *The Emergence of the African-American Art: Robert S. Duncanson, 1821-1872*. Columbia and London: The University of Missouri Press, 1993), pp. 11-12. However, the oral history account of Duncanson's father as a white Scottish-Canadian, and his mother a Negro, originated in the early twentieth century by FC (Francis Carr) Wright, an amateur historian in the town of Mt. Healthy, Ohio, and first published in an article by Conteur, "Robert S. Duncanson, A Cincinnatian Who Became World Famous as an Artist," in the *Cincinnati Enquirer* (December 12, 1924), p. 1. James A. Porter subsequently published this information in his article "Robert S. Duncanson: Midwestern Romantic-Realist," *Art in America* 39, no. 3 (1951), pp. 99-154, the first monographic study of Duncanson, and the story still circulates, most recently in John Wilmerding's essay, "Reflections on the American Landscape," *Wall Street Journal* (September 25, 2010). In addition, there is no consistent evidence as to his precise birth date. By consensus of the largest number of primary resources, I have established his birth year as 1821. See Ketner, op. cit., p. 13, footnote 8, pp. 208-9.

12 An important piece of primary information was discovered by Julie Aronson, Curator of American Art, Cincinnati Art Museum, that notes Duncanson's middle name as "Seldon," not "Scott," as is often cited, and confirms the early biography of the artist. See "Artists and the Fine Arts Among Colored People," *Repository of Religion and Literature* (Indianapolis, Indiana), v. III, no. 1 (January 1860), p. 3. No other primary resource notes Duncanson's middle name. The attribution of "Scott" to the "S" in Duncanson's name is a twentieth century construction built on the myth of the artist's Scottish-Canadian white father. David Driskell first mistakenly published Duncanson's middle name as "Scott" without footnoting the reference for this information in his *Two Centuries of Black American Art* (New York: Alfred A. Knopf/Los Angeles County Museum of Art, 1976), p. 38.

13 "Artists and the Fine Arts Among Colored People," op. cit.

14 Reuben and Martha Graham were also "free colored persons," who were from Virginia suggesting that they were family friends of the Duncansons and indicating the tight-knit social network among "free colored persons."

15 *Detroit Daily Advertiser* (February 2, 1846), p. 2.

16 Ketner, op. cit., p. 34-35.

17 Robert S. Duncanson to Junius R. Sloan, January 22, 1854, Spencer Papers. Newbury Library, Chicago.

18 Asher B. Durand, "Letters on Landscape Painting, VIII," *The Crayon* 1, no. 23 (June 6, 1855), p. 355.

19 Thomas Cole, "Sicilian Scenery and Antiquities," *Knickerbocker* (March 1844), p. 244.

20 *Ball's Splendid Mammoth Pictorial Tour of the United States. Comprising Views of the African Slave Trade, of Northern and Southern Cities, of Cotton and Sugar Plantations of the Mississippi, Ohio and Susquehanna Rivers, Niagara Falls, &c.*. Cincinnati: Achilles Pugh, Printer, 1855. Cincinnati Historical Society, Ohio, np.

21 "Henry Box Brown's Mirror of Slavery," Boston: 1850. See John T. Kneebone, et al, eds., *Dictionary of Virginia Biography*. Richmond: The Library of Virginia, 1998, 2: 294-6. William Wells Brown's Original Panoramic Views of the Scenes in the Life of an American Slave, from his birth in slavery to his death or his escape to his first home of freedom in British soil" (London: Published by Charles Gilpin, 1850).

22 Ketner, op. cit., pp. 102-4.

23 Robert S. Duncanson to Junius R. Sloan, August 21, 1854, Spencer Papers, Newbury Library, Chicago.

24 See my extended interpretation of the painting's significance in Ketner, op. cit., pp. 112-13.

25 Moore, Thomas, Lalla Rookh: An Oriental Romance. London: Longman, Hurst, Rees, Orme, and Brown, 1817.

26 *Cincinnati Weekly Gazette* (October 22, 1862), p. 2.

27 Nickerson, Cynthia D. "Artistic Interpretations of Henry Wadsworth Longfellow's *The Song of Hiawatha*, 1855-1900," *The American Art Journal* v. 16, no. 3 (Summer 1984), pp. 49-77.

28 Kleeblatt, Norman L. "Master Narratives/minority artists," *Art Journal*, v. 57, no. 3 (Autumn 1998), p. 29.

29 *Daily Cincinnati Gazette* (November 24, 1865), p. 2.

30 "*The Land of the Lotos-Eaters*. Painted by R.S. Duncanson," *Art-Journal* (London), n.s., v. 5 (1866), p. 93.

31 Ketner, op. cit., p. 175.

32 Du Bois, op. cit., p. 5, 6.

33 Du Bois, op. cit., p. 12.

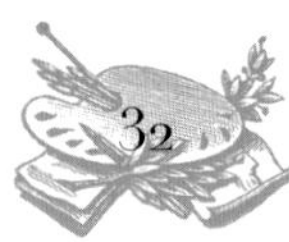

Exhibition Checklist

Hunting in the Woods, 1846, oil on canvas, 12 ¾ × 18 ½ inches. Dr, Dianne Whitfield-Locke, Mitchellville, Maryland.

Summer, 1849, oil on canvas, 11 ½ × 16 ⅜ inches. Michael Rosenfeld Gallery, LLC, New York, New York.

Carp River, Lake Superior, 1850, oil on board, 8 × 10 inches. Private Collection.

Landscape, 1851, oil on canvas, 15 × 22 inches, Collection of the Hunter Museum of American Art, Chattanooga, Tennessee, Museum purchase, HMAA. 2007.6

Time's Temple, 1854, oil on canvas, 34 × 59 inches. Howard University Gallery of Art, Washington, DC.

Ball's Mammoth Pictorial Tour of the United States. Cincinnati, Ohio: Archilles Pugh, 1855. Facsimile courtesy Cincinnati Historical Society, Ohio.

Richard Sutton Rust, 1858, oil on canvas, 30 × 25 inches. Richard S. Rust IV, Cincinnati, Ohio.

The Temple of the Sibyl, 1859, oil on canvas, 35 × 50 inches. Springfield Museum of Art, Ohio.

Allegorical Figure, 1860, oil on canvas, 28 ⅞ × 36 inches. Alexander Gallery, New York, New York.

Untitled (Landscape), c. 1860-65, oil on board, 7 ½ × 9 ½ inches. Dr. Ronald & Mrs. Patricia Walters, Silver Spring, Maryland.

Western Landscape, 1861, oil on canvas, 9 × 15 inches. Private Collection.

Untitled, 1861, oil on canvas, 19 ½ × 31 ½ inches. Michael Rosenfeld Gallery, LLC, New York, New York.

Minnehaha Falls, 1862, oil on canvas, 20 × 16 inches. Howard University Gallery of Art, Washington, DC.

Vale of Kashmir, 1863, oil on canvas, 9 × 16 inches. David Hausrath, Fort Thomas, Kentucky.

Vale of Kashmir, 1870, oil on canvas, 26 × 49 ¼ inches. George Wein, New York, New York; Courtesy of Michael Rosenfeld Gallery LLC, New York, New York.

Mountain Pool, 1870, oil on board, 14 × 11 inches, Kenkeleba House, New York, New York.

Scottish Landscape, 1871, oil on canvas, 20 × 36 inches. William Rybolt, Cincinnati, Ohio.

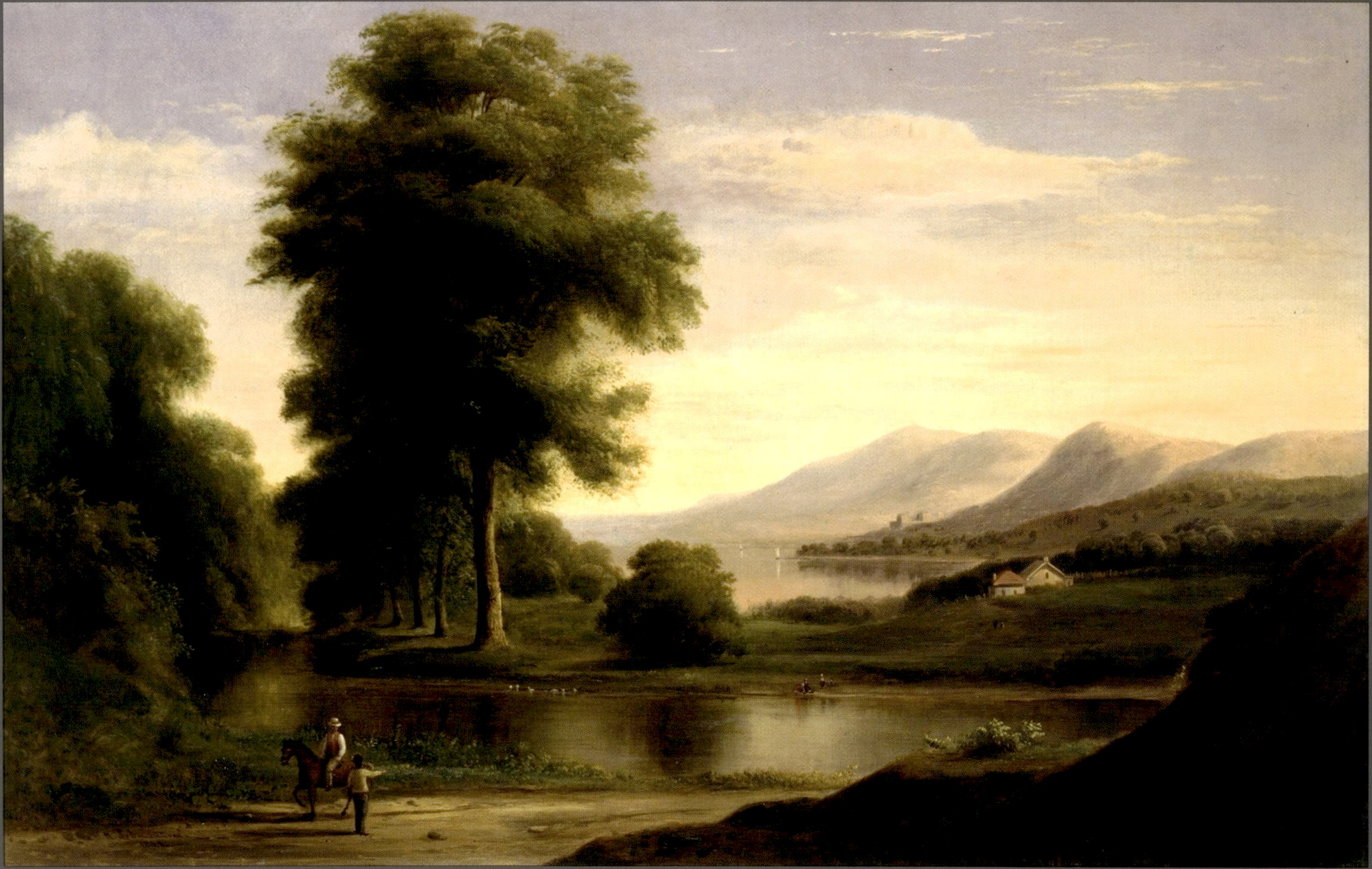

Fig. 29. Robert S. Duncanson, *Untitled*, 1861, oil on canvas, 19 ½ × 31 ½ inches. Michael Rosenfeld Gallery, LLC, New York, New York.